Ben Jonson and Self-Love

Φιλαυτία.

Ben Jonson and Self-Love

The Subtlest Maze of All

Robert Wiltenburg

UNIVERSITY OF MISSOURI PRESS
COLUMBIA AND LONDON

Copyright © 1990 by
The Curators of the University of Missouri
University of Missouri Press, Columbia, Missouri 65211
Printed and bound in the United States of America
All rights reserved

5 4 3 2 1   94 93 92 91 90

Library of Congress Cataloging-in-Publication Data
Wiltenburg, Robert Edward, 1947–
   Ben Jonson and self-love: the subtlest maze of all / Robert Wiltenburg
    p. cm.
   Bibliography: p.
   Includes index.
   ISBN 0-8262-0717-0 (alk. paper)
   1. Jonson, Ben, 1573?–1637—Criticism and interpretation.
2. Self-love in literature. 3. Self in literature. 4. Love in
literature. I. Title.
PR2642.S38W55 1989   89-4842
822'.3—dc20   CIP

∞™ This paper meets the requirements of the
American National Standard for Permanence of Paper
for Printed Library Materials, Z39.48, 1984.

Designer: Liz Fett
Typesetter: Connell-Zeko Type & Graphics
Printer: Thomson-Shore, Inc.
Binder: Thomson-Shore, Inc.
Type face: Sabon

Frontispiece illustration from Andrea Alciati's *Emblemata* (1621) courtesy of
Phillip Mills Arnold Semeiology Collection, Special Collections, Washington
University Libraries, St. Louis.

For Candace

CONTENTS

Preface ix

I
Of Nature in Men 1

II
Volpone the Lover 21

III
Epic and Epigram 45

IV
The Subtlest Maze of All 91

Epilogue 124

Bibliography 129

Index 149

PREFACE

The current revaluation of Jonson has produced some important contributions to our understanding of the plays, the masques, and the poems, yet we have hardly begun to succeed in seeing him whole. Perhaps we never will. Difficulties arise not only from the range, complexity, and contradictions of the personality and the work, but also from the critical compartmentalization that has often (and often to good purpose) focused on some element of Jonson: the satiric dramatist, the masque-maker, the neo-stoic moralist, the neoclassical lyrist, and so on. My own interest in Jonson began when I happened to be reading, at the same time, his poetry in one context and his plays in another. Impatient of these divisions, I wanted to account for, if not to unite, his contrary excellences in dramatic and nondramatic poetry. This book is the product of that attempt, one which will, I hope, despite its own inevitable partiality, be useful to others who choose to wander in the rich flood of Jonson's art.

My first question was formal: How are the concerns and techniques evident in the plays related to those in the poems? It soon became entwined with a second, thematic question. The poet being, Jonson observes in *Forrest* I, "bound to reherse" "Some act of *Love's*," can we even imagine, as Joseph Summers has asked, a major Renaissance poet who could not? That the experience of love is also fundamental to Jonson has been demonstrated in part by Anne Barton's account of its "return" in the late plays. I argue here that it is present in one form or another throughout and that Jonson's evolving artistic response to the problems posed by love and, more particularly, by self-love helps to shape his divergent achievement in drama and poetry.

One must begin, as Jonson did, with self-love. The idea was relatively new (the *OED* cites a first use in 1563), and Jonson explored it more intently and continuously than any of his contemporaries. As Edmund Wilson once acutely (albeit unsympathetically) suggested, *Cynthias Revels* (or, *The Fountain of Self-Love*) may be said to present the essential materials from which Jonson's whole career developed. Wilson's analysis of a "morose" Jonson gets at something important, but in the wrong way, unnecessarily ascribing to Jonson himself the least attractive peculiarities of his characters. Writers do of course contain their fictions, and one who returns repeatedly to certain characters and patterns betrays, if not a guilty secret, an obsessive concern—or so this hedgehog of an artist may appear to a polymathic fox of a critic.

That Jonson is first and last an artist is still the most important observation to be made about him. For all his learning, he is neither a profound nor a systematic thinker, nor one who much changed in what he saw and thought. Rather, he lives most in that rare energy invested in the treatment of his materials, in the aemulous conversation with his literary predecessors, in the continual search, lasting even until the end of his life, for still better means with which to "instruct men in the best reason of living." In the light of such a purpose, the artist's obsession is to genius near allied. The "narrowness" of which Wilson complains is also the source of Jonson's greatest virtues, the concentration with which he returns, and the determination with which he penetrates, to the fundamental issue of Renaissance (and modern) individualism: the centrality of self-love and its effects in the economy of psychic and social life. This is the foul rag-and-bone shop in which Jonson works. How is self-love to be understood? How is it to be controlled or civilized? How can it be cultivated to produce the rarer fruits of willing obligation, of friendship, of freedom, and of love?

Thus the "subtlest maze" of love and self-love. My general argument is that Jonson's increasing mastery (and separation) of dramatic and nondramatic forms goes hand in hand with his maturing treatment of self-love and the civilizing responses to it. This is not to suggest that the question of self-love and its treatment provides an all-subsuming, explanatory key to Jonson. With an artist so rich and various, there can of course be no such thing. But it does provide a continuing thread in the fabric, an essential point of reference from which to estimate his diverse efforts and achievements.

The subject is a large one, here treated emblematically rather than exhaustively. I begin with Jonson's initial presentation of the problem of self-love in *Cynthias Revels*, the first work in which the formal and thematic elements of his mature art are held in uneasy tension. I then turn to *Volpone* for the quintessential expression of Jonson's sense of the dramatic character of evil: the brilliance, corrosive power, wanton self-destruction, and final pathos of a self-love that would separate "nature" from "fortune."

Having examined the challenge of self-love in two plays, I consider the proposed countermeasures in the two poetic collections Jonson completed. The *Epigrammes*, both in their form and in the performance of the omnipresent speaker, provide paradigms for the civilizing responses to self-love and for the unpretentious heroism those responses require. Taken together with *Volpone*, the *Epigrammes* demonstrate the separation of materials necessary to the fullest, most effective expression of Jonson's dichotomous moral and aesthetic vision: evil sinuous, continuous, and dramatic; good occasional, incremental, best discovered in arrested moments of amusement or awareness. Finally, *The Forrest* explores the need not only for friendship but for love, and the variety of loves that may flourish once self-love has been bound—at Penshurst, in marriage, and through poetry—and confesses the necessary incompleteness of the transformation of self-love to love while in man's "state."

Wiser in his art than in his life, wiser for others than for himself, Jonson's own story is, despite significant achievements and consolations, not a particularly happy one: there is always some melancholy in his mirth, and little calm of mind, even at the close. So much greater therefore is the temptation—which I have not entirely resisted—to create critical fictions with endings more perfect than any Jonson permitted himself. That we feel moved to do so testifies to the continuing power of his art, divided as it is, to strike at something deep (and deeply divided) in ourselves.

In the course of this work I have acquired debts of many kinds. I have been materially assisted by research grants and a semester's leave from Washington University. Much is owed to teachers and friends at the University of Rochester and to colleagues and friends at Washington University for instruction, conversation, and encouragement. I am particularly obliged for help on specific points to Linda Flowers and Frederick Locke, and for close scrutiny of the whole—including much sound advice—to Cyrus Hoy, Mary Ann Radzinowicz, and Susanne Woods. Clair Willcox of the University of Missouri Press has improved almost every page. Of Joseph Summers, who has been present from the beginning, I can only say as Jonson said of Camden, that to have been his student is to be his friend—rare privileges both.

All quotations of Jonson are from the edition of C. H. Herford and Percy and Evelyn Simpson, *Ben Jonson*, 11 vols. (Oxford: Clarendon Press, 1925-1952), abbreviated as H&S. I have modernized the use of i/j and u/v.

Ben Jonson and Self-Love

Chapter I
Of Nature in Men

The title of Francis Bacon's thirty-eighth essay, "Of Nature in Men," still contains, in its modest antique precision, a vital idea. We are accustomed to bits of talking and thinking ("human nature," "the nature of man," "man in nature") in which "nature" is ever the substance or location and "man" merely the qualifier or temporary occupant.[1] However sound the reasons, both historical and practical, for our concern with the question of man's place in nature, we must recognize that this question did not interest the Renaissance in quite the same way. Bacon's phrase testifies that man was not always the minor premise. Nature had not yet been reduced to mere mechanism, nor expanded to an all-embracing condition, and perhaps cause, of human life. It was a source of analogy, not explanation, existing on a plane of metaphysical dignity hardly equal to human experience.

Beyond the probability of historical anachronism, concern for the Renaissance "problem" of man's place in nature seems more fundamentally misconceived. To adapt Samuel Johnson, natural philosophy vexes no man.[2] Speculations regarding the nature of the physical world, though sometimes delightful and of some practical importance, are of no ultimate concern except insofar as we choose to enter into them imaginatively and use them as metaphors to explore our fears and hopes. What does it matter (except to an astronaut) whether the earth circles the sun or vice versa? Whether the final constituents of matter are waves, particles, or something yet undreamed of? Our cosmic malaise or sense of sin may be projected equally well upon a Ptolemaic cosmology—the corrupt earth as dead center and

---

1. I follow here, for simplicity, Bacon's use of "man" and "men" to signify *humanity*.
2. Boswell reports Johnson's remark that "publicke affairs vex no man" (*Life of Johnson*, 15 May 1783).

sinkhole of the universe—or upon a modern one—the earth an insignificant particle swimming in the infinite void. Our hopes of redemption are equally derivable from the firm order and purpose beyond the moon or the superior civilization of some unknown galaxy. The vehicle changes but the tenor remains; the trepidation of the spheres is indeed innocent. What mattered for the Renaissance is what mattered for Socrates and still matters for us: not man in nature, but nature in man.

Bacon's little essay is organized as a series of Senecan forays in and around aspects of his subject: an objection or two, a linking summary, a bit of practical advice, a limited simile, an embracing metaphor. Yet this multiplicity and apparent discontinuity of rhetorical tactics do not make it any the less beguiling a miniature, nor prevent the formation of distinct impressions of what nature is and what can be done with it. The essay expresses with great clarity both a "vision" and a "judgment"; that is, a vision of the way things are or can be and a judgment of the ways in which particular actions, habits, ways of thinking and acting contribute to either state of affairs.[3]

Bacon begins with a powerful summary of the case:

> Nature is often hidden; sometimes overcome; seldom extinguished. Force maketh nature more violent in the return; doctrine and discourse maketh nature less importune; but custom only doth alter and subdue nature.[4]

As often in Bacon, the matter and manner are here intimately connected.[5] The first sentence presents a wonderfully tight compression of elemental conflicts: seen and unseen, victor and vanquished, light or fire and darkness or cold. These are arranged in a counterpointed double sequence of diminishing frequency ("often, sometimes, seldom") and increasing effect ("hidden, overcome, extinguished") in which the metrical value of the "time" words is held constant (all trochees) to suggest the steadiness of the observer, while that of the "action" words is carefully augmented (trochee, anapest, amphibrach) to suggest the increasing difficulty of the action described. Thus, the first sentence suggests that, based upon observation, man's relation to the nature within him is one of elemental, unremitting struggle the outcome of which is rarely (and then only with difficulty and at

---

3. The terms are Gabriele Bernhard Jackson's (*Vision and Judgment in Ben Jonson's Drama*, 2–3).

4. *The Works of Francis Bacon*, 6:469.

5. See Stanley Fish's discussion of Bacon's literary method in ch. 2 of *Self-Consuming Artifacts: The Experience of Seventeenth Century Literature*.

great length) favorable. The second sentence presents a dramatic expansion, again in three parallel clauses, of the preceding "vision" and moves to a "judgment" and recommendation to action. The method is to expand backwards to discover the causes of the previously observed effects: *force*—which sounds rather like itself; *doctrine and discourse*—a nice discrimination; and the unassuming hero of the sentence, *custom*. Three attempts are made upon nature. The first "maketh nature more" and the second "maketh nature less," but as the parallel constructions indicate, the differing results obtained by force and reason are less important than their similarity as temporizing, unsatisfactory measures. One aims too low, the other too high successfully to encounter and subdue nature. Enter the humble *via media*, custom. Notice that the third term in this series represents more than the extrapolated third term of the first sentence. Although the general form of the third clause is similar to the two preceding (it is one of the choices), the parallel is broken within the clause by the substitution of "alter" and "subdue" for the "making" of force and reason. Only custom can "alter," that is, make other, recreate, while the others merely "make," that is, shape or influence the existing.

Why custom? The answer gleams through Bacon's method. He begins with the present ("Nature is") fruits of observation (the three past participles); he then moves from the observed effects to their causes (force, doctrine and discourse, custom), which are stated in a way that provides a basis for future choice. Bacon thereby executes a complex temporal maneuver in which, firmly anchored in the present, he manages to glance significantly at both past and future. This is a common strategy in the literature of the time.[6] But the dynamism of Bacon's conception of the nature "within" is remarkable. Nature is neither substance nor quality, but a ceaseless activity, defining itself by what it does.[7] As nature is dynamic, the adequate response of the understanding and the will must also be continually shifting, defining, qualifying itself in action. Therefore, both scientist and moralist require custom, the little agent of habitual attention, thought, and action, always adapting itself to shifting motive and circumstance, meeting nature on her own protean grounds, and subduing her to its own quiet, regular purposes—as neither force nor reason will do.

So much can Bacon say in a little. Two sentences give us all the

---

6. See Lowry Nelson, *Baroque Lyric Poetry*, 19–40.
7. See Pico della Mirandola, "Oration on the Dignity of Man," 223–25; also Thomas Greene, "The Flexibility of the Self in Renaissance Literature."

essentials, and the method of presentation is congruent with the content: we move from compressed observation to an enlarged understanding, which is in turn the basis for future actions that will provide the material for further observations, understandings, etc.—an endlessly dynamic calculus of the adequate response.

The end of the essay is as instructive as the beginning; for if Bacon comes in like a scientist, he goes out like a poet. As the first sentences impress with their magisterial acuity and condensed weight, the last strikes us with its homely images: "A man's nature runs either to herbs or weeds; therefore let him seasonably water the one, and destroy the other."[8] The metaphor precisely consolidates the analysis of natural dynamism: seeds in the personality—inclinations, desires, passions—continually present themselves, grow, and attempt to dominate. As he says earlier, "nature will lay buried a great time, and yet revive upon the occasion or temptation."[9] It is a source of perpetual possibility, perpetual confrontation and choice, demanding continual vigilance. (We might remember that, according to Milton, even the prelapsarian gardeners had their hands full.) And the response must be "seasonable"; that is, recurrent, fitted to the time, not once and for all, but a habitual awareness, judgment, choice, and activity.

Yet this image gives more than a metaphoric reiteration of the opening analysis. It holds out to the wise gardener a promise of use and beauty hardly suggested at the beginning. It implicitly assures us that the business of mastering nature, though toilsome, is not arcane; though it may be in this world the essential struggle, involving ultimate questions of health or disease, yet it remains a matter of everyday experience, requiring everyday solutions. The nature that counts, the nature "within," though powerful and usually destructive, is still subject to consciousness and moral agency—of which all are capable, however seldom they may rise to that capacity.

Bacon's view of "nature in men," its dynamism, its present danger, its rare promise, is similar in many ways to that of Ben Jonson. Jonson was, of course, Bacon's sincere admirer. He toasted him publicly in a poem written on the occasion of Bacon's sixtieth birthday as "the wisdome of my King."[10] In the relative privacy of the *Discoveries,* he reserved his highest praises for Bacon's eloquence ("the marke, and ἀχμὴ of our language" [923]) and his learning ("a wise Patriot," notable for his "care of the *Common-wealth* of

---

8. Bacon, *Works,* 6:470.
9. Ibid., 470.
10. *The Under-wood,* LI.20. All quotations of Jonson are from C. H. Herford and Percy and Evelyn Simpson, *Ben Jonson,* hereafter abbreviated as H&S.

Learning" [924–26]), and copied in the opinion of the Venetian Fr. Fulgenzio Micanza that "hee seem'd to mee ever, by his worke, one of the greatest men, and most worthy of admiration, that had been in many Ages" (941–43).[11] Bacon's and Jonson's views are not identical, but they do share a vision both of man's natural predicament and of his possible responses to it. That predicament Jonson explores initially in *Cynthias Revels* and exposes most vividly in *Volpone;* the possible responses, Baconian and otherwise, are most fully developed in the *Epigrammes* and *The Forrest*.

* * *

We are not accustomed to thinking of Ovid in connection with Jonson. Of course Jonson knew him and used him incidentally often enough, but compared with his debts to other Roman authors, Ovid has never seemed to bulk very large. The evidence suggests, however, that he was particularly on Jonson's mind in 1600–1601, at the threshold of Jonson's major work. He figures in both of the plays entered for that year: as a character in *Poetaster,* and less directly, though to greater effect, in *Cynthias Revels,* the first considerable work in which Jonson begins to address the question of "nature in men" in ways that prepare the ground for the major poetry and plays.

Gabriele B. Jackson, in her persuasive analysis of *Poetaster,* has argued that in Jonson's ongoing examination of the proper relation of imagination to action, of poetry to society, Ovid is "weighed in the balance and found wanting." She finds in the play neither a merely conventional Renaissance estimate of the hierarchy of literary genres, nor a simple-minded evocation of a golden (or rather, silver) age of literature in contrast with the thankless present, but a testing of the poets against the ideal of a public, "socially motivated" poetry practiced by Virgil and Horace. Ovid is shown to be perverse, using his divine gift for profane and private ends. Jackson sees in him the sinister and fascinating coincidence of "good poetry" and "bad ethics" that Jonson later examines in the characters of Mosca, Subtle, and Catiline.[12]

Yet the negative judgment on Ovid in *Poetaster* refers mainly to Ovid the love poet; the more significant use (for our purpose) of Ovidian material in *Cynthias Revels* draws upon the "epic" poet of the *Metamorphoses*.[13]

---

11. For the extended passage in the *Discoveries,* see H&S, 8:590–92; for Fr. Micanza, see the editors' comments, 11:244.

12. Jackson, *Vision and Judgment,* 20–30.

13. See Brooks Otis, *Ovid as an Epic Poet,* especially ch. 3; Louis L. Martz, *Milton: Poet of Exile,* pt. 3; Richard J. DuRocher, *Milton and Ovid,* especially 20–29.

Academic critics have sometimes not known quite what to make of the *Metamorphoses;* even a flurry of recent interest has not quite altered their slightly disreputable reputation. Poets, however, have used them freely, especially the story of Narcissus and Echo, which has always been among the most frequently imitated, adapted, and commented upon of all the tales.[14]

Jonson responded particularly to this story, and makes of it his only extended use of Ovidian material.[15] We might recall that *Cynthias Revels* was originally entered on the *Stationer's Register* as *Narcissus, or the fountain of self-love,* that the fountain is given pride of place on the title page of the Quarto, and that it is still remembered on that of the Folio. While it is impossible to reconstruct the process of the play's composition, the Narcissus material clearly retained in Jonson's mind a significance disproportionate to its dramatic function. He treats the episode with extraordinary care; for while one must agree with C. H. Herford that the mythic episode is "undeveloped" in terms of ordinary dramatic articulation, it must be recognized that Jonson made of it a delicate but compelling piece of poetry.[16]

Jonson is not content merely to extract the Narcissus story from Ovid, but uses it as the central panel in a triptych of Ovidian references; thus framed, it becomes the controlling emblem of the play.[17] The scene is nominally the "vale of Gargaphie," mentioned in Ovid as sacred to Diana and containing the pool at which Actaeon discovered her bathing (*Meta-*

---

14. See Louise Vinge, *The Narcissus Theme in Western European Literature up to the Early 19th Century;* also Kenneth J. Knoespel, *Narcissus and the Invention of Personal History.*

15. There are, of course, many occasional citations; see H&S, 11:654.

16. See the substantive and textual introductions in H&S, 1:393-412, 4:3-23. Interpretation of the changing title reveals a rift in the customary unanimity of the Oxford editors. Herford seems inclined to take the earliest entry as an indication of Jonson's concerns and intention at some stage of the project (1:399); the Simpsons state flatly that "The confused form in which the title is entered on the Register cannot have come from Jonson; Narcissus is not even a character in the play" (4:3). This seems to go too far. Even if the form of the title is not Jonson's, he is nonetheless the source of it; though Narcissus is not a character in the play, he figures prominently in it.

17. Joseph Loewenstein has also observed that "Echo . . . preside[s] over the play's ritual center . . . until displaced by . . . Cynthia" (*Responsive Readings: Versions of Echo in Pastoral, Epic, and the Jonsonian Masque,* 5). I think this is quite right, but am not persuaded that she earns this "centrality" by presenting a "myth of cultural memory" (5), or by raising "the problem of imitation" (77), or by displaying "the pathos attendant on the invention of a self constructed out of the words of others" (92). Jonson's Echo seems more straightforward and more moral, raising questions not of authenticity and imitation (more our problem than Jonson's) but of love and self-love.

morphoses, 3.156). In the play, however, the stories of Actaeon, Narcissus, and Niobe all occupy parts of this same moral and poetic ground. All three are drawn from that section of the Metamorphoses (3.1–6.400) that Brooks Otis has called "the avenging gods"[18] —though for Jonson the proper word is "justice" rather than "vengeance" (see *Cynthias Revels,* I.i.93–94). The references to Actaeon and Niobe (3.138–252, 6.146–312) provide two simpler stories that complement each other and establish a moral spectrum on which we place Narcissus and Echo.

What does provoke the gods and invite destruction? Actaeon, the young hunter, becomes his own victim when he unwittingly attempts more than is permitted. Niobe is an old woman who deliberately boasts the superiority of her children to those of the goddess Latona. Their punishments fit their natures and their crimes: the unwary boldness of Actaeon dispersed, torn apart; the conscious defiance of Niobe immobilized in stone. Yet innocent error and deliberate folly are each less common and less interesting than the mixed nature and fate of Narcissus. Like Actaeon, he has a fatal vision; not of the goddess, the forbidden divine, but of himself and of his own beauty. Like Niobe, he boasts of his self-sufficiency and defies not a goddess but his fellow men, rejecting not divine piety but human love. As his faults are on a human scale, so is his changing awareness of his situation more interesting to our sympathies. In Ovid the advantages of this human myth are turned to ironic purpose. The story of Narcissus is set as an episode in the story of Tiresias and establishes his credentials as a prophet. Within this frame, Ovid constructs a delicious irony: "When Tiresias was asked whether this child would live to reach well-ripened age, the seer replied: 'If he ne'er know himself'" ("si se non noverit") (III.346–48).[19] This irony is later compounded in the climactic scene (442–73) in which Narcissus bemoans his fate and comes to know his image, if not himself: "Oh, I am he! I have felt it, I know now my own image" ("Iste ego sum; sensi, nec me mea fallit imago") (463). He has previously "seen" without "knowing" himself, and now when recognition has finally come, he is too weak from "dolor" to act upon it, and settles instead for an autistic *Liebestod:* "we two shall die together in one breath" ("nunc duo concordes anima moriemur in una") (473). Here we have an exquisite Ovidian damnation: seeing, he did not know, knowing, he cannot act. All that remains is to suffer beautifully and to submit with whatever grace the gods or the poet permit.

Jonson, ever the practical moralist, could not rest here. He chooses to

---

18. Otis, *Ovid as an Epic Poet,* ch. 5.
19. For text and translation of Ovid's *Metamorphoses* I have used the Loeb edition.

focus on the story of Echo, a choice which is not so odd when we remember that Narcissus and his avatars are everywhere present in the play. Moreover, it is Echo, the respondent to self-love, even as later it is Crites, the responding "discoverer" of the court's passionate vanities, who makes all the difference. Vanity and self-love one must take for granted as part of the irreducible substrate of nature in men; Jonson directs our attention to the possible countermeasures.

Although Ovid was apparently the first to fuse the tales of Narcissus and Echo, he makes Echo hardly more than a sympathetic bystander, ill-used, long-suffering, and ineffectual, who lacks even the negative significance of causing Narcissus' downfall. It is the curse of an earlier suitor that invokes the Nemesis that overtakes him.[20] Yet Jonson's Echo also contrasts with other Renaissance moralizations of the character. In contemporary interpretation she ranges from the "reflex of God's spirit, the voice of God" that can lead the soul to heaven, to Bacon's understanding of her as one of those who flatter the "proud, fastidious, and disdainful" Narcissus into his "infernal" solipsistic retirement.[21] Jonson's version is closer to Beatrice than to her antitype, but his Echo is beyond allegorization, remaining delicately and convincingly herself. Jonson does not idealize. He retains the characteristic garrulity that got her into trouble with Juno in the first place as an irritant for the kindly but impatient Mercury (and for the audience impatient for the promised sports to come). Nor is her view more comprehensive than her situation warrants. Like other "idle worldlings," she is still too apt to "Censure the powers above" (I.ii.94-95).

Despite these limitations, she does, as Calvin Thayer has observed, seem "to establish the artistic basis of the play" by representing the "archetypal sufferer from the follies of self-love."[22] (This is perhaps not quite accurate because it excludes the suffering of the self-lover, but in general true enough.) To expand Thayer's comment: as her suffering makes her the

---

20. For the assertion that Ovid was the first to fuse these elements, see Dewitt T. Starnes and Ernest William Talbert, *Classical Myth and Legend in Renaissance Dictionaries*, 197.

21. Vinge, *Narcissus Theme*, 382, n. 36; Bacon's interpretation appears in *De Sapientia Vetera* (1609), translated (1619) by Sir Arthur Gorges (Spedding, Works, 6:705-6). Vinge cites Farra (1594), Heinsius (1639), Reynolds (1632), and George Herbert (1633) in giving the positive view. For Boccaccio's interpretation of her as "true fame," see Starnes and Talbert, *Classical Myth*, 197-98. For the negative view, Starnes and Talbert cite Berchorius (1484) and others; for both positive and negative side by side (*Responsive Readings*, 88-89), Loewenstein cites Charles Estienne's *Dictionarium Historicum* (1553).

22. Calvin G. Thayer, *Ben Jonson: Studies in the Plays*, 35.

moral basis of the play, the beautifully refined affection of her speeches and song, contrasting with the brilliantly perverse intellectual preciousness of the courtiers, makes her the aesthetic basis as well. She has, Jonson tells us, been waiting three thousand years to have her say, so we should not be surprised to find she says it well. And her authority is strengthened by the circumstances of her coming. She arises from the earth itself (a more solid basis than that of other characters in the play), and comes on the authority of Jove, which is greater even than that of Cynthia. Further, her words are the product of a natural growth. Thus, she hopes that she "may be delivered / Of the prodigious griefe" (21-22) that has so long grown inside her.

Her speech divides into three parts: the initial monologue (18-53) and prelude to the Song (with Mercury); the Song (65-75); and reflections on the Fountayne (with Mercury) and the curse (76-105). The first two parts, preparation and lament, are the most important. The monologue recollects and judges her experience and Narcissus' fate. It is cast in regular blank verse with heavier end-stopping than Jonson often uses, and its chief ornaments are apostrophe and query (both often providing an initial stress), parenthesis, and toward the end, irregular rhyme. This form conveys both her intended calm and her actual distress, which manifests itself as an incomplete mastery of the situation (apostrophe and query) and of her own emotions and actions (parenthesis and irregular rhyme). The "unconscious" or "uncontrollable" breaking into rhyme (38-39, 43-44, 49-50, 52-53), which comes more quickly at the end, suggests that something is about to be born, that a statement of even greater formality will be necessary to express adequately the depth of her emotion.

What can be the content worthy of such care? In the relation of Echo and Narcissus, actual and potential, Jonson gives us, in a compressed, embryonic form, his view of the difficulties posed by "nature in men" and an indication of the appropriate response. Echo begins by describing Narcissus as, like Actaeon, his own victim ("trophae of self-love, and spoile of nature") and as perpetually contemplating, like Niobe, his mistake (26-29). But the heart of her speech deals with what should have been:

> Had ECCHO but beene private with thy thoughts,
> Shee would have dropt away her selfe in teares,
> Till shee had all turn'd water, that in her,
> (As in a truer glasse) thou might'st have gaz'd,
> And seene thy beauties by more kind reflection:
>
> . . . .

> Why did the gods give thee a heav'nly forme,
> And earthy thoughts, to make thee proud of it?
> Why doe I aske? Tis now the knowne disease
> That beautie hath, to beare too deep a sense
> Of her owne selfe-conceived excellence.
> O, hadst thou knowne the worth of heav'ns rich gift,
> Thou would'st have turn'd it to a truer use,
> And not (with starv'd, and covetous ignorance)
> Pin'd in continuall eying that bright gem,
> The glance whereof to others had been more,
> Than to thy famisht mind the wide worlds store:
> "So wretched is it to be meerely rich.
> Witnesse thy youths deare sweets, here spent untasted,
> Like a faire taper, with his owne flame wasted.
>
> (31-35, 40-53)

Echo proposes a theory of two "mirrors" in which one may choose to see oneself: the mirror of mere nature which, like Narcissus' pool, returns an image too simply true of the self in isolation—an image that lacks the definition and correction of a human context and that we can neither recognize nor use; or the mirror of love and human interaction, the "truer glasse" that gives a "more kind reflection."[23] This second mirror is more "kind" in several senses. It is more beneficent than indifferent nature, it is more "natural" because it leads to fertility and propagation of the human personality in action, and finally, it reawakens "kindness" in the Shakespearian sense, that essential kinship and mutual obligation which makes healthy action possible and inevitable suffering tolerable. That one of these mirrors must be chosen is never in doubt. In rejecting Echo and his other suitors, Narcissus rejects the potentially redemptive reality that our actions resonate or "echo" in other lives. It is only through this resonance that we come to know truly and use wisely the "beauties" we have been "given."[24]

---

23. Cf. Spenser, *Amoretti*, XLV, 1-4:

> Leave Lady in your glasse of christall clene,
> Your goodly selfe for evermore to vew:
> and in my selfe, my inward selfe I meane,
> most lively lyke behold your semblant trew.

24. Starnes and Talbert take a very different view of Echo's character. Although admitting that Jonson "seems to have been familiar with the various interpretations of the Echo myth and to have attempted to mold them into a coherent whole" (*Classical Myth*, 200), they believe this is accomplished by subordinating the positive interpretations to an identification of her as Iactantia (boasting) to Narcissus' Philautia (self-love). Thus, they take her

As a word alone may signify but cannot mean, so one alone may see but cannot know the self. Both need to be implanted in the fertile soil of a sentence or a poem, of an action or a love.

The alternative is both unnatural ("selfe-conceived excellence") and self-destructive. Thus he remains "starv'd" and "ignorant" amid his own wasted "riches" and "sweets"; neglecting the "truer" use of his own real goods, his "famisht mind" craves "the wide worlds store." This touch is entirely Jonson's—no such elements appear in Ovid—and is characteristic. The motif is developed later in this play in Phantaste's speech (added in the Folio) at IV.i.171-215, where she celebrates the joys of narcissistic love in a variety of "shapes": "I would ever bee follow'd with th'affections of all that see mee. Mary, I my selfe would affect none" (190-92). This motif forms the kernel of some of Jonson's greatest characters—Volpone, Sir Epicure Mammon, Catiline—all of whose famished minds and fevered imaginations (Phantaste) ransack the world for things and experiences to fill the void left by the absence of love. Like Narcissus, each fails to find his proper "food" and ends "with his owne flame wasted."[25]

Consider what a change from Ovid's version this shift to Echo's (and, of course, Jonson's) perspective has accomplished. Narcissus' situation has lost nothing of its poignancy, nothing of the horror of his self-immolation, but it has lost its point—or rather, its original point has been gathered into a more comprehensive view of man's nature and prospects. Where Ovid is artistically sensational and philosophically resigned, Jonson is probing, scientific, and hortatory. Despite his reputation as a "rough satirist" whose delight it is to blame and punish the unworthy, he is more compassionate than Ovid.[26] He damns no one. As the fifth act will demonstrate in detail, all, though subject to reproof, are capable of reform. Some increase in self-knowledge and some bettering of behavior is always possible, though never inevitable. Yet his optimism is not simple. The interest and difficulty of

---

"truer glasse" speech (31-35) as an example of improper boasting and tie it to her later complaints against Cynthia (82-92), producing an unambiguous vice. I think rather that the discordant elements in her character reflect an emotional and psychological realism that draws equally on both traditions, the allegorized virtue and vice, to produce a portrait of a love that is flawed but vital.

25. If, as Herford and Simpson believe, this speech of Phantaste's was written at the time of the Quarto, Jackson's interpretation (*Vision and Judgment*, 30) of Ovid in *Poetaster* as the turning point in Jonson's treatment of the imagination needs revision.

26. On Jonson's "compassion," see, among others, Alvin Kernan, *The Cankered Muse: Satire of the English Renaissance*, and Joseph A. Bryant, Jr., *The Compassionate Satirist: Ben Jonson and his Imperfect World*.

errors of nature—failures to know one's nature, one's true good, with the consequent misplacing of affections and desires—lie in the fact that such errors are usually at least half right. Beauty *is* desirable, and a sensitivity to it has often been thought both a natural insight into and affirmation of the goodness of the created world, as well as a precondition for intellectual and moral progress.[27] Narcissus' devotion to beauty is more right than wrong, but his ignorance of beauty's nature and use proves fatal. Echo now begins the process of reorienting that misdirected love.

Narcissus himself is, of course, already beyond the pale. As in any elegiac situation, it is the reader who remains to be educated, and the masterly "Song" (65-75) now moves to involve him more directly. It is "melodramatic" in the best sense of that unfortunate word. It is, in the first place, a highly wrought expression of a powerful emotion which wars against (or appears to war against) the very structure that gives it form; second, it is literally musical. Mercury has commanded:

> Begin, and (more to grace thy cunning voice)
> The humorous aire shall mixe her solemne tunes,
> With thy sad words: strike musicque from the spheares,
> And with your golden raptures swell our eares.
>
> (61-64)

The standard objections to melodrama—that it involves strained emotionalism (language and gesture such as men do not use) and a sense of hovering and interfering deity (the organ music of the soaps)—are here overruled by the material itself. In the interplay of mythic characters, we are invited to witness a closer encounter than is ordinarily possible between human desire and a divine reality whose purposes, though opaque to "idle worldlings," are nonetheless sympathetic and harmonious. Echo's "sad words" will mix with the "solemne" "musicque from the spheares" to produce as full a statement as possible of this situation, and inferentially, of the human condition.

Would that we had the original music.[28] But even without it, the song

---

27. See, for example, Mark Rose, *Heroic Love: Studies in Sidney and Spenser*, ch. 1. For the extent and importance of the Narcissus story in the Renaissance, see Vinge, *Narcissus Theme*, and Douglas Bush, *Mythology and the Renaissance Tradition in English Poetry*.

28. The nearly contemporary setting for three voices by Henry Youll (*Canzonets to Three Voyces*, 1608) can have only a problematic relation to a song designed for one. Mary Chan, in her discussion of music in the play (*Music in the Theatre of Ben Jonson*, 45-63), suggests the possibility that Youll has simply added two lower parts to the original solo song.

impresses with its blended quiet and energy, its complementary impulses to dissolution and control. The diction and imagery are of a familiar elegiac sort: *slow, slower, faintly, gentle, heavy, weepes, droupe, fall, melting snow, drop, wither'd.* We seem to have one more watery lament in which the speaker is nearly overwhelmed by waves of grief. Yet always in the best elegies there is present an activity, an insight, an effort of mind and will that resists, even as it acknowledges, the power of dissolution. Usually this resistance leads, if not to a full acceptance, to a determination to continue. However, the rhetorical purpose here is a little out of the ordinary. While fully expressing the grief, its movement is not to return the speaker to the business of living and striving—for she is a figure of myth—but to regather her into the artifice of eternity, leaving her song as an emblem and warning. Instead of the epitaphic "Reader, stay," we begin with the slowing of the fountain to "keepe time" with Echo's tears. The point is not to effect a reflective pause for the restless mind, but a temporary harmony between the continually upwelling "freshness" of nature and the "salt" tears that result when that water is filtered through experience. The next two lines ("List to the heavy part the musicque beares / Woe weepes out her division, when shee sings") prepare for the song within the song that follows, while expanding and sharpening our sense of the "division" to be mourned. The source of the music is, after all, the same heaven that sustains the fountain, even as the human capacities for love and pain sustain the flow of tears. Echo now proceeds to her central insight, contained in three brief, sententious, heavily rhymed lines that give us at once the simplest and most widely ramifying statement of Narcissus' and her own significance:

> Droupe hearbs, and flowres;
> Fall griefe in showres;
> "Our beauties are not ours.
> (69–71)

It sounds conventional: still another evocation of the sympathetic despondency of nature in the face of human pain, plus a pat moralization. But if we look more closely, we see that the first line recalls the Narcissus of line 26 ("this drouping flowre"), while the second describes Echo herself, who has wished (21–22) to be "delivered" of her "prodigious griefe," and whose tears may be conventionally described as falling showers. Thus, the appeal to the natural world turns out to be an appeal to Narcissus and herself, who are themselves no more than further forms of nature's selfless self-expression. If we are not substantially ourselves, that is, clearly differentiable from the natural continuum, surely nothing so accidental as our "beauties" can be ours either.

We see then how well Jonson has understood and, to a point, agreed with Ovid. No matter what the Platonist or the Neoplatonist may claim for the dignity and special state of man, he remains Adam still, a metamorphosing bit of the metamorphic rhythms of nature and time. In isolation he is but a drooping flower defined by his appearance, by a conjunction of qualities he uses but did not make and cannot control any more than the flower does.

But having reached this central point the voice breaks and changes:

> O, I could still
> (Like melting snow upon some craggie hill,)
> drop, drop, drop, drop,
> Since natures pride is, now, a wither'd daffodill.
>
> (72-75)

The strain of the willed harmony and insight of the preceding lines has been too much to sustain, and her passion overflows in broken interjection, a sharp figure, and the daring line of drops which seem to hit more slowly, fully, and heavily, until we reach the bottom of her grief, and are ready for the concluding hexameter. Again we must admire the piquancy and restraint of Jonson's treatment of this situation. He concludes but does not close, maintaining the impulses toward balance and imbalance throughout. The balanced content ("natures pride" vs. "wither'd daffodill"; past vs. present) amplifies the earlier "divisions" of "fresh" and "salt" and the rest. Yet the problem remains open through the imbalance of the form. One might expect the strong medial caesura of a final hexameter, but where is it? Instead, we find an elongated pause on the word "now" which not only breaks the expected symmetry, but also makes clear why the satisfactions of symmetry are here inappropriate.[29] The problem persists: unlike the strictly human elegy which celebrates and completes one cycle as it ignites another, the mythic elegy exists in an enduring present that underlies and continually breaks in upon human life.

It comes as no surprise then that the scene is not tied off neatly and quietly, but ends with Echo's mutterings against Diana—which reveal that her insight is limited by self-pity and by a pity for Actaeon and Niobe that forgets justice—and her supererogatory curse on the fountain. The wrangling with Mercury is complemented by Amorphus' blundering pursuit;

---

29. On Jonson's characteristic asymmetry, see Jonas A. Barish, *Ben Jonson and the Language of Prose Comedy*, especially 71-77.

she, and what she represents, must remain available to man, though eluding the grasp of the unworthy.

While one may agree with Thayer that Echo is in some sense the "artistic basis of the play," the claim needs qualification. She is the affective response to the problem of self-love, but for Jonson, as for Bacon, moral choices are never simply a matter for the emotions or will, but require the critical intelligence that belongs in this play to Cynthia and to her agents, Arete and Crites. Echo has shown us the tragedy of those who feel, and now Cynthia must give us the comedy, at least the happier ending, of those who think.

Between Echo in Act I and Cynthia in Act V, Jonson has provided an extensive, often witty, sometimes pedantic "discovery" of the "antic and ridiculous" forms self-love may assume in and around a court. This satire comprises the bulk of the play's incidents though it has no organic relation to the essential, mythic action of the play: the setting and the solving—built, respectively, around Echo's song and the "Hymn to Cynthia"—of the problem of self-love.[30] Being primarily examples of the problem and passive beneficiaries of the solution, the courtly characters contribute little to this action. Yet they do play a significant role in the audience's understanding of self-love, which is more often encountered in forms comic and ridiculous than tragic and self-destructive. The qualities of Hedon and Anaides, of Philautia and Phantaste, are all, fortunately, more common than those of Narcissus. Moreover, our perception and judgment of these comic social avatars of Narcissus are developed by continually seeing them through the eyes of Crites and Arete, who measure them against the best that men and women may be, and of Mercury and Cupid, who take ironic delight in observing and punishing (with laughter) their "prodigious follies." Only after this extended education in the school for self-love are we ready for the resolution to be offered via hymn and masque, that all "May be converted on workes, fitting men" (V.iv.640).

The fifth act opens (in the Quarto) with the "Hymne to Cynthia," and, as is often the case, the more artificial the linguistic object, the closer it comes to the heart of the matter. Perhaps the first thing to notice is that it is exactly what it claims to be: a hymn, pious and celebratory, and liturgical in its means. It gracefully fulfills the mythic and social requirements of the occasion; it compliments the queen while faithfully employing the dual tradition of Diana as stern huntress and virgin.

30. Herford and Simpson discuss the differences between the Quarto and Folio texts in H&S, 4:17-22. Great swatches of the satire are added or subtracted without much effect on the whole.

But the poem's ambitions and successes seem to lie deeper still. It is as perfect an evocation of pure reason—quiet, sentient, luminous—as could be imagined, and proposes that we celebrate the night and its sovereign not merely as a break in the normal course, but as an alternative "state," a "day of night" that contrasts in every important way with the ordinary "day of day." In this contemplative state, almost nothing is happening, largely because of Jonson's careful control of verbs and verb forms. The poem has scarcely a transitive verb, but abounds in infinitives, past and present participles, statements of customary or determined behavior, and ritual imperatives (keep, bless, give) that require attitudes rather than actions. The agents (Cynthia, Earth, Hesperus, and formerly, the Sun) are large, separate, and act upon each other, if at all, at a distance, by interposition, entreaty, or influence.

After the invocation and the "state" it establishes, we have stanzas dealing with Diana as queen, her nocturnal beneficence, and her place in the universal scheme, and with Diana as huntress, her diurnal manifestation, and its danger to man. In the second stanza, the timely admonition of the hierophant speaker forestalls any possible interruption by the earth of this wished-for state. But in the third stanza the equilibrium, though not upset (these are, however, the only fully enjambed lines in the poem) is quickened and set vibrating—or, to use William V. Spanos's word, "resonating"[31]—by the striking introduction of the "flying hart":

> Give unto the flying hart
> Space to breathe, how short soever.
> (V.vi.15–16)

Amid this quiet ritual celebration lurks a tremor of arrested activity. It is not discordant; the image works mythically and dramatically. The hunt is proper to Diana, and the image glances at Actaeon, whose punishment has been defended as just throughout the play. Now, however, the diseases of self-love having been exposed and their masquerade as virtues about to be, it is a time for healing mercy.

Yet the image remains disturbing. It reminds us of the world of pain and fear that the elaborate ritual repose of Cynthia's "state" has been constructed to avoid. It reminds us that this peace is a short respite snatched from the perpetual chase. It reminds us of our place in this little drama of

---

31. William V. Spanos, "The Real Toad in the Jonsonian Garden: Resonance in the Nondramatic Poetry," 1–23.

the poem. For, of course, we are the hunted, ours the flying heart (surely the pun must be admitted) that pursues and is pursued by what we "love." That the heart should be "in flight" is exactly right, for Jonson perceives that the incessant search for fresh experience, pleasure, and affections (here again we must think of the great gourmands would-be he later creates) is often little more than a glorious cover for the flight from self-knowledge and one's true good. The flying heart is the emotional counterpart of the famished mind.

We might also at this point remember Jonson's motto, "Tanquam explorator." This phrase has suggested to some that Jonson conceived of himself as a sort of literary Francis Drake, but an examination of the full context in Seneca (*Moral Epistles,* 2.5-6) reveals an important assertion of method. Defending his studies in his philosophical rival, Epicurus, Seneca remarks: "soleo enim et in aliena castra transire, non tamquam transfuga, sed tamquam explorator" ("for I am wont to cross over even into the enemy's camp, not as a deserter, but as a scout").[32] Thus, the motto implies that what is done matters less than the manner and purpose of the action; so also, we now find, with self-love. The masquelike revels provide a transition point, a pause that gives new direction to the promptings of nature, the ever-welling fountain of self-love. Here we discover something Echo could not show us: the problem is less self-love *per se* than self-love wrongly conceived and applied. The eighteenth century was not the first to discuss "self-love" as a positive quality, the precondition of a sound mind. Juan Luis Vives, one of Jonson's favorite neo-Latin authors, whose *Introductio ad Sapientiam* (1524; English translation, 1540) served as an Elizabethan schoolbook, remarks: "To love oneself is to essay, to work, to seek, and to strive with great prayers to God so that our most excellent part, the mind, might be adorned and cultivated with true brotherhood and ornaments, especially religion."[33] True self-love is the love not simply of the self as it is or appears to be (Narcissus' error), but of what is best about the self and what it may become. The former leads to indolence or feverish exhaustion, solipsism, and death, the latter to health, self-knowledge, and integration into the true moral, social, and metaphysical order. As Pope has it, "True SELF-LOVE and SOCIAL are the same."[34]

Before the purified vision of self-love can be presented, the ground must

---

32. All quotations and translations are from the Loeb edition of Seneca's *Epistulae Morales*.
33. Vives' *"Introduction to Wisdom: A Renaissance Textbook*, 155.
34. Alexander Pope, *An Essay on Man*, 4.396.

be cleared of the imperfections which limited Echo's view. This Cynthia proceeds to do in the speech that follows the "Hymne":

> Such is our chastitie: which safely scornes
> (Not *Love,* for who more fervently doth love
> Immortall honour, and divine renowne?
> But) giddie CUPID, VENUS franticke sonne.
> (51-54)

Now we are ready for the first masque, in which Cupid, "like ANTEROS," presents "foure faire virgins from the palace of their Queene *Perfection*" (V.vii.3-4), the first of whom is self-love:

> The first, in citron colour, is *naturall Affection,* which given us to procure our good, is somtime called STORGE, & as every one is neerest to himselfe, so this hand-maid of reason, *allowable selfe-love,* as it is without harme, so are none without it: Her place in the court of *Perfection* was to quicken mindes in the pursuit of honour. Her device is a *perpendicular Levell,* upon a *Cube,* or *Square.* The word, SE SUO MODULO. Alluding to that true measure of ones selfe, which as everie one ought to make, so is it most conspicuous in thy divine example. (26-35)

This self-love, purified by a self-knowledge more precise than the "truer glasse" of Echo's affection, in turn gives rise to the other social and moral virtues that comprise "Perfection": "pleasant Conversation," "well conceited Wittinesse," "Simplicitie," and then, in the second masque, "elegance," "fine humour," "hardy courage," and "good nature." All that remains is Cynthia's formal discovery of the masquers as mere impersonators of the virtues they present, their "poenance" of a "palinode" (V.xi.141-43), and their dismissal

> to the well of knowledge, *Helicon*;
> Where purged of your present maladies,
> (Which are not few, nor slender) you become
> Such as you faine would seeme: and then returne,
> Offring your service to great CYNTHIA.
> (V.xi.153-57)

They will render "service" in a double sense, returning to do better homage to Cynthia and confirm the vision of the last act, and opening outward to the larger world as the final song directs:

> Now each one drie his weeping eyes,
> And to the well of knowledge haste;
> Where purged of your maladies,

> You may of sweeter waters taste:
> And, with refined voice, report
> The grace of CYNTHIA, and her court.
>
> ("Palinode," 35-40)

What conclusions does this examination suggest? It does not, I think, indicate a need for any revaluation of the play that would reassign it to a place of greater prominence in Jonson's dramatic canon. The implications of its relatively static problem-and-solution structure for Jonson's handling of longer poetic forms lie less in the direction of his mature dramaturgy than in that of the "antimasque" and "masque" arrangement of his court entertainments and in the looser rhythms of a collection like the *Epigrammes*. In short, there seems no reason to disturb the consent of centuries that the play, considered as a play, is scarcely more than an "interesting failure."

Yet this analysis should heighten our interest and suggest some reasons for the failure. It is, in the first place, remarkable that we should find Jonson's mature understanding of the "nature in men"—self-love as the spring and motive of all human action and the emotional and intellectual forces that may direct it to a healthy end—so fully articulated (albeit schematically) in so early and imperfect a work. We have here almost all the elements of the moral psychology that Jonson later explores in *Volpone, The Alchemist, Catiline,* and the *Epigrammes*.[35] At the same time, however, Jonson presents this moral vision almost without benefit of drama. Granting his skilled observation and witty dialogues in the satiric sketches of the courtiers, one cannot escape the fact that the significant developing "action" (such as it is) is carried primarily by the exquisite poetic set pieces we have examined. The play thus demonstrates T. S. Eliot's general observation that Jonson possessed "not so much skill in plot as skill in doing without a plot."[36]

---

35. Judith Kegan Gardiner similarly observes that "*Cynthia's Revels* is the most profound and thorough study of the psychology of narcissism in the English Renaissance, and it reveals themes central to Jonson's later development" ("'A Wither'd Daffodill': Narcissism in *Cynthia's Revels*," 40).

36. Eliot goes on to say that "what holds [a] play together is a unity of inspiration that radiates into plot and personages alike" (*Essays on Elizabethan Drama*, 75-76). The idea is developed in Ray L. Heffner, Jr., "Unifying Symbols in the Comedy of Ben Jonson."

Loewenstein remarks on the play's "paratactic dramaturgy" and on a "pattern of generic rivalry between masque (*Cynthia's Revels*) and satire (*The Fountayne of Selfe-Love*)" (*Responsive Readings*, 78, 85); L. A. Beaurline speaks of "two conflicting forces . . . one moving toward the contemplation of an exalted ideal . . . the other . . . attacking self-love" (*Jonson and Elizabethan Comedy: Essays in Dramatic Rhetoric*, 121). E. M. Thron discerns three elements: myth, character satire, and masque ("Jonson's *Cynthia's Revels*: Multiplicity and Unity," 235-47).

Plot may be, as Aristotle said, the soul of tragedy; or, as Francis Fergusson amends Aristotle, an "action" may be the soul of both tragedy and comedy.[37] Jonson's imaginative embodiment of his "vision" produces rare poetry (surely the author of the "Hymne to Cynthia" was already at or near the height of his poetic powers) but not an "action." In what follows, I will argue that much of Jonson's vision remained essentially undramatic, that his great success in drama resulted less from the finding of his proper form than from the careful selecting and limiting of his materials and that consequently much of what is most important in Jonson lies in the non-dramatic poetry.[38]

As we have seen, the abstract and rarefied literariness of *Cynthias Revels* has its fragile beauties. In the following chapters we will examine *Volpone* and the *Epigrammes* to discover what happens when Jonson turns his attention to providing, in ways more accessible to ordinary experience, a dramatic presentation of nature's "problem" and a poetic presentation of man's "solution."

37. See Francis Fergusson, *The Idea of a Theater*, ch. 1 and the appendix "Plot and Action."
38. Kernan has also, though to a different end, examined the "undramatic" quality of Jonson's vision. See his discussion of *Volpone* and "The Nature of Plot" in *The Plot of Satire*.

Chapter II

Volpone the Lover

In pairing *Volpone* with the *Epigrammes,* one risks an embarrassing confrontation, for *Volpone* of all Jonson's works has pleased the most readers, while the *Epigrammes* seem to have pleased Jonson best.[1] But the two belong to the same imaginative and poetic world: Jonson successfully embattles similar virtues and vices in each and gives substantial life to the moral insights sketched in *Cynthias Revels.* Yet when they are compared, it will be seen that Jonson had good reason for his high opinion of the *Epigrammes.* The differences of form and strategy applied to essentially similar materials produce a complementarity that approaches, in purity of effect, that of antimasque and masque: *Volpone* presents Jonson's fullest exposition of the evils that beset humanity; the *Epigrammes,* the "ripest of my studies," his vision and enactment of the good still possible.

Volpone has from the beginning given fits to generically minded critics and would-be comfortable readers, who have found its richly textured language, allusions, and intrigue oddly able to elude their nets and surprise their expectations. Nor is this effect limited to readers and spectators of the play; even the Avocatori, the judges on the scene, are bewildered by the richness and complexity of the possibilities. Jonson, while calling the play a "Comoedie," felt it necessary to discuss its divagations from the "strict rigour of *comick* law" in the dedication to the universities originally prefixed to the Quarto. There he makes his well-known defense of the poet and of stage poetry by defining the "office of a *comick-Poet:* to imitate justice, and instruct to life, as well as puritie of language, or stirre up gentle

---

1. If we may judge by the dedication of the *Epigrammes* to William, Earl of Pembroke, his most important patron, and the claim that they represent "the ripest of my studies" (H&S, 8:25).

affections."² Yet Jonson was also at pains to disarm the critical sense that there is something odd about the play. He locates possible objections in one's sense of the ending, the most obvious and, as he thinks, most easily defended point of critical attack.³ He pleads both the example of the ancients, "the goings out of whose *comoedies* are not alwaies joyfull" (118-19), and his own determination "to put the snaffle in their mouths, that crie out, we never punish vice in our *enterludes,* &c" (115-16). But even the best apologies are little more than patches over some tear that cannot be mended. The recourse to reason and precedent may aid but cannot control our experience of the play, and whether we are inclined to judge of genres by analytic or historical criteria, or by some sophisticated amalgam of the two, *Volpone* remains something of a puzzle. While respecting Jonson's general designation of the play as "comedy," I think it is still necessary to inquire more closely into what sort of play this is and what its primary concern is.

The acrostic "Argument" prefixed to the play in imitation of Plautus, though it sorts well enough with the comparison to the seriousness and dignity of the ancients that Jonson presses in the dedication, comes as something of a surprise. Jonson was hardly fond of the form, including it with others regarded as overly elaborate among the "serious follies" to which he pleads innocent in "An Execration upon *Vulcan*" (*Under-wood*, XLIII.33-41). Yet Jonson masters even that which he despises. In his single nondramatic use of the form, he produced the touching epitaph "On Margaret Ratcliffe" (*Epigrammes,* XL). In the present example (and in the similar one prefixed to *The Alchemist*), he not only manages to describe the action of an exceptionally busy play, but also to capture the salient rhythms of the action as well, making of the poem a microcosmic play and of the play a macrocosmic poem:

> V OLPONE, childlesse, rich, faines sicke, despaires,
> O ffers his state to hopes of severall heires,
> L ies languishing; His Parasite receaves
> P resents of all, assures, deludes: Then weaves
> O ther crosse-plots, which ope' themselves, are told.
> N ew tricks for safety, are sought; they thrive: When, bold,
> E ach tempts th'other againe, and all are sold.

---

2. H&S, 5:121-23.

3. The ending still provokes widely divergent interpretations. John Creaser, for example, sees Volpone as "in full command" at the end ("*Volpone*: The Mortifying of the Fox," 353), while Stephen J. Greenblatt finds him still struggling to cover "emptiness, boredom, the void" ("The False Ending in *Volpone*," 93).

"Volpone, childlesse, rich. . . ." Two adjectives suffice to characterize him, and were this all we knew of Volpone, it would be nearly all we need to know to assess his moral situation, particularly in light of the example of Narcissus, who in Echo's words:

> Pin'd in continuall eying that bright gem [his beauty],
> The glance whereof to others had been more,
> Than to thy famisht mind the wide worlds store:
> "So wretched is it to be meerely rich.
> (*Cynthias Revels,* I.ii.48-51)

For all its varied brilliance, the play is largely devoted to deepening and extending our appreciation of the oxymoronic force of those primary adjectives. They do of course define the main action of the play, legacy hunting, that Jonson has taken over from hints in several classical authors, and they do so with the mordant economy of Martial. But Volpone's "childlessness" is more than an enabling premise; it suggests the dimensions of his real isolation, the sterile, perhaps maimed, condition that has cut him off from the flow of life, even as his "richness" indicates the illusory plenitude with which he deceives and is deceived.[4]

After pausing on these adjectives, the poem rushes headlong in a torrent of verbs (averaging two per line) to the momentary catch at the end of line six ("When, bold") before falling over into the final action ("Each tempts th'other againe") and the epigrammatic judgment ("and all are sold"). This corresponds closely to the main rhythms of the play. The initial adjectives reproduce the relatively leisured introduction of the opening scene. The rushing, intermingled transformations from "faines" to "thrive" give us the main action of the play up to the point when, in apparent safety, Volpone and Mosca undertake through sheer "wantonness" their final temptation, are discovered, and "sold." The last word picks up and completes the "rich" of the first line. Volpone's childlessness, however, is not similarly tied off and lingers as a pervasive comment and question.

Yet this is not just an epigram (even in Jonson's rigorous understanding of the term), but also an acrostic, and the acrostic form requires a peculiar intimacy between the subject and the action described. The letters of

---

4. S. Musgrove observes that "parent-child relationships [were] to an Elizabethan . . . not merely social relationships, but inherent and vital parts of the whole universal system [of nature]" (*Shakespeare and Jonson*, 28). Lawrence Danson notes that "'Childlesse' is the first quality assigned to Volpone, even before 'rich,' because the childlessness gives the richness its special twist" ("Jonsonian Comedy and the Discovery of the Social Self," 187).

Volpone's name beget each line of the developing action of the poem, even as in the play everything derives from Volpone, his house, his situation, his activities. He is mainspring and motive. What he is and does, and what others do and become with respect to him, are at the focus of a centralized concern which, for its all-gathering intensity, is rare even in so notoriously "centralizing" an artist as Jonson. Not even *The Alchemist* presents so compelling a vortex of imagination, action, and effect.

This formal integrity sharpens the second critical question: what is the central concern embodied in Volpone and his fate? There have been many suggestions. E. B. Partridge makes much of the elements of parasitism and bestiality; L. C. Knights traces the corrosive effects of individualism and capitalism on the stable feudal order of social relations; Alvin Kernan and Thomas Greene find here the demonic underside of Pico's promise of man's nearly infinite plasticity; John S. Weld and Harriet Hawkins, noting Jonson's use of Erasmus, see an exploration of the nature and effects of folly.[5]

Each of these approaches is helpful in its way, but I think one aspect of the play has been neglected. Swinburne, whose comments, though sometimes reckless and always extravagant, are often useful, felt that there was "a savour of something like romance" about *Volpone*.[6] And it seems to me that *Volpone,* like most great stories, is primarily a love story, albeit a love gone (and going) very badly wrong. Its generic mode, if it must have one, is that of frustrated romance, and its "plot" is the presentation of Volpone as false lover—false in two senses: as one who loves the wrong things and one who loves the right things in the wrong way.

The play opens with Volpone's morning hymn, blasphemy and idolatry abounding:

> Good morning to the day; and, next, my gold:
> Open the shrine, that I may see my *saint*.
> Haile the worlds soule, and mine. More glad then is
> The teeming earth, to see the long'd-for sunne
> Peepe through the hornes of the celestiall *ram*,
> Am I, to view thy splendor, darkening his:

---

5. Partridge, *The Broken Compass: A Study of the Major Comedies of Ben Jonson*; Knights, *Drama and Society in the Age of Jonson*; Kernan, Introduction to *Volpone*; Greene, "Ben Jonson and the Centered Self"; Weld, "Christian Comedy: *Volpone*"; Hawkins, "Folly, Incurable Disease, and *Volpone*."

6. Swinburne, *A Study of Ben Jonson*, 35: "there is in *Volpone* a touch of something like imagination, a savour of something like romance, which gives a higher tone to the style, and a deeper interest to the action."

> That, lying here, amongst my other hoords,
> Shew'st like a flame, by night; or like the day
> Strooke out of *chaos,* when all darkenesse fled
> Unto the center. O, thou sonne of SOL,
> (But brighter then thy father) let me kisse,
> With adoration, thee, and every relique
> Of sacred treasure, in this blessed roome.
>
> (I.i.1-13)

Jonson, a moral psychologist rather than a theologian, is here concerned less with the abuse of religious language than with the cosmically projected narcissism that makes the defilement of the temple possible. Such idolatry requires in the first place a radical oversimplification of human nature and psychology. That a man should treat as primary reality, as the touchstone of all life and activity, some product of his own mind or of the collective mind of his culture is no less astounding for being common. But Jonson, serious and orthodox though he is, is no "precise, illuminate brother" given to self-righteous denunciations. Instead, he gives narcissistic folly its head (and a very eloquent voice) even as he has his characters, in the midst of their boasting, trace a correcting perspective that suggests their eventual undoing.[7] They begin to work out their own destruction in our minds long before they do so in fact, and one of the great accomplishments of the play lies in the skill with which the latent significance of their words is gradually, inevitably, made manifest.

Jonson establishes a pair of moral coordinates in the opening line: "Good morning to *the day;* and, next, *my gold*" [my emphasis]. We see at once two lights, two possible orders of experience and activity analogous to Echo's two "mirrors": the public (definite article/natural good) and the private (possessive pronoun/conventional good)—what Mosca will shortly generalize as "nature" and "fortune." Which is to have authority? Which is the primary reality that compels our attention and allegiance?[8] Yet even the introduction of the conflict suggests the lines of force that will determine the final, "comic" resolution. Nature must ultimately be served, just as it is

---

7. On the language of folly, see Beaurline, *Jonson and Elizabethan Comedy,* ch. 5.

8. In his edition of the play, R. B. Parker cites the traditional distinction between "the innate gifts of Nature and the chance gifts of Fortune" (*Volpone or, The Fox,* 98) and in his introduction adduces Luther's remark that "Money is the word of the *Devil,* through which he creates all things, the way God created the true world" (31). Cf. Alexander Leggatt, *Ben Jonson: His Vision and Art,* ch. 1, on the "false creation" of "secondary worlds" in *Volpone* and elsewhere.

immediately served (despite the inversions) in Volpone's speech; even the highest praises of his gold are comparative, derivative, secondary. This is also the mark of Volpone's imagination, the habit of mind that sets him somewhat apart from Mosca throughout. The revolution, the symbolic parricide he so blithely announces ("O, thou sonne of SOL / [But brighter then thy father]"), is self-consciously wicked—a learned perversity that pays implicit homage to the better even in the act of embracing the worse. Mosca's wickedness is, in comparison, less complicated psychologically, though infinitely various in its execution.[9] Jonson skillfully suspends these elements in solution, giving the knaves the best lines and most of our sympathy, giving us the momentary thrill of being of the devil's party (and knowing it), while assuring us of its ultimate (self-)defeat.

We soon see the ramifications of this conflict between nature and fortune, the resonance for Volpone of "childlesse, rich." It appears that he is to be fatherless as well as childless—that is, entirely cut off from the access to grace, the first step in the perfection of love, that the natural affections provide (as we have seen in the treatment of Storge in *Cynthias Revels*). Volpone's next lines explicitly extend this isolating revolt from the cosmic and natural realms to the social:

> Thou being the best of things: and far transcending
> All stile of joy, in children, parents, friends,
> Or any other waking dreame on earth.
>
> (16–18)

For Jonson, the problem of moral evil is that it is so much easier, more immediate, efficient, coherent, and "reasonable" than the incremental, laborious difficulty of goodness. It has an almost pastoral appeal, for it partakes, as does the pastoral, of what William Empson has called "putting the complex into the simple."[10] Indeed, Volpone shortly provides us with an account of his methods that refers to a precivilized, infantile golden age

---

9. On the particular quality that differentiates Volpone from the other characters, even Mosca, compare Weld's observation that "The power of the play . . . derives not from the demonstration that Volpone is a fool, but from the demonstration that he is a wise man who is a fool" ("Christian Comedy: *Volpone*," 186). R. B. Parker notes that the name "Musca" (fly) was applied not only to parasites, but also to demonic familiars, and that in the beast fables, the fox as false preacher is sometimes accompanied by an ape assistant (*Volpone or, The Fox*, 17, 21).

10. William Empson, *Seven Types of Ambiguity*, 23. On the contemporary use of pastoral to "obfuscate" social and moral conflicts, compare Louis Adrian Montrose, "Of Gentlemen and Shepherds: The Politics of Elizabethan Pastoral Form," 432. At its best, the pastoral works instead to explore such issues.

in which one may gain without labor.¹¹ But the difference between true pastoral and this parodic "pastoral of evil" lies in the nature of the simplifications each effects. True pastoral simplifies the objects of experience (kings become shepherds; the cares of state, sheep) while preserving the dynamics. It simplifies the elements the better to perceive the complexity of their relation, the energies existing between them. But Volpone's and Mosca's proposed "pastoral" vision is just the reverse, retaining the objects (children, parents, friends, money, and the rest) while simplifying the dynamics. As Mosca so aptly puts it: "Riches are in fortune / A greater good, then wisedom is in nature" (28–29). Thus we have the major premise that fortune and nature are separable orders of experience, that it is possible to live in one and not the other. The minor premise (although it consumes more space in the drama) is that the order of fortune is superior to that of nature.

One can scarcely imagine a fuller challenge to everything Jonson stood for as poet and moralist. Much of his best poetry in celebration of the nobility addresses itself particularly to the complex interactions of nature and fortune as they take shape within the primary social unit of the family. For it is within the family that the claims of nature and fortune, of affection and power, of mutual obligation and individual assertion come to their ripest conflict.¹² Jonson has here, in Nietzsche's words, "found his proper enemy" and is determined to give this demi-devil his due. Volpone and Mosca propose for themselves and effect for their victims the dissolution of all those relations that tend to keep life human; that is, of those paradoxical structures of moral identity (here, for example, the citizen, the father, the husband) in which the self becomes richer and more productive through constraint—as in language, where a word is useful only when defined.¹³ Once these bonds are broken, there beckons an infinitely degrading metamorphosis, ending only in the final constriction or in the stultification and polymorphous sterility so finely imaged in the grotesques, Volpone's puta-

11. This should give pause to those who, like Raymond Williams (*The Country and the City*, 32–33), tax Jonson with ignoring the cost of labor in "To Penshurst."
12. Steven Ozment has similarly observed that "historians best understand the early modern family at the crossroads of values and structures, where freedom meets necessity, ideals confront nature, and minds self-consciously choose" (*When Fathers Ruled: Family Life in Reformation Europe*, vii).
13. Annabel Patterson refers to "the self—deliberately revealed as committed to and complicit in society, and only *therefore* conscious of autonomy" ("Lyric and Society in Jonson's *Under-wood*," 160).

tive children, and in the entertainment (Mosca's "invention") they perform in scene ii.[14]

Volpone's complex situation is presented with great subtlety. He feels that he has committed himself fully to the realm of "fortune," but we see that he cannot entirely free himself from the claims of "nature." He continues to want the things men commonly want:

> Thou [his gold] art vertue, fame,
> Honour, and all things else! Who can get thee,
> He shall be noble, valiant, honest, wise—
> (25–27)

Now whether he actually wishes to possess these things or would merely be reputed to have them is immaterial. Here and elsewhere he describes his desires in terms of public or publicly acknowledged, natural goods—including sensual pleasure—while Mosca, his less noble but more ingenious coadjutor, is ever at hand to suggest and to exacerbate the desire for more private, abstract, grandiose (and ultimately illusory) pleasures. Thus, as Volpone is reciting these genuine virtues, Mosca interrupts:

> And what he will, sir. Riches are in fortune
> A greater good, then wisedom is in nature.
> (28–29)

Similarly in the next scene (I.ii), after the entertainment, as they discuss the impending visit of Voltore, Mosca refers to the "great, and learned Advocate" (108). Volpone, his mind appearing to wander, replies, "Yes, to be learned, Mosca." Mosca quickly responds:

> O, no: rich
> Implies it. Hood an asse, with reverend purple,
> So you can hide his two ambitious eares,
> And, he shall passe for a cathedrall Doctor.
> (110–13)

Mosca continually reduces and undermines Volpone's half-remembered, half-forgotten vision of the good, recalling him to their shared demonic

---

14. Greene describes the play as "an anatomy of metamorphosis . . . the infinite, exhilarating, and vicious freedom to alter the self at will once the ideal of moral constancy has been abandoned," the "cruel lesson" of which is that "gold fails to confer that infinite mobility its lovers covet, but rather reduces them to the status of fixed, subhuman grotesques" ("Ben Jonson and the Centered Self," 337, 343).

ideal (best expressed in the soliloquy opening Act III) of an infinite plasticity and power, an ironic superiority to all men, all conditions, all experience.

Volpone imagines that he alone among men can "gaine no common way" (I.i. 32-33), can separate fortune from nature. It is an illusion that civilization makes plausible and that city life (temporarily) supports.[15] And he claims to be superior even to the profitable game he and Mosca have been playing:

> I glory
> More in the cunning purchase of my wealth,
> Then in the glad possession.
> (I.i. 30-32)

Yet this pretended superiority and self-sufficiency is qualified in two ways as soon as the action begins. There is in the first place the paradoxical spectacle of Volpone's feigned (physical) and real (spiritual) impotence, together with the dazzling alternations between the images of the gloating ironist and the immobile, grasping, physically disgusting voyeur of Mosca's sprightly machinations. Even more significant, both for the ending and for the overall interpretation of the play, is the emotional quality of his relation to Mosca. Volpone frequently offers to embrace or kiss him, even at one point wishing him a "Venus" for greater intimacy. The natural desire for affection peeps through the perverse expression of it, revealing a Volpone not quite so self-sufficient as he would like to imagine.[16]

* * *

Given this opening, how do we end up with dramatic action having a rise, crisis, resolution, reversal, and judgment, instead of an exposition of the knaves and fools, tempters and tempted, on the order of *Cynthias Revels* or *Every Man Out of His Humour*? In fact, the first two acts seem to point in the direction of just such an allegorical and satiric exposition.[17] Their carefully modulated procession of birds (vulture, raven, crow), moral identities (citizen/orator, father, husband), and crimes (against the common good, against pious succession, against the marriage bond) is more expository than dramatic. False lovers themselves, Volpone and Mosca act as a

---

15. See Gail Kern Paster, *The Idea of the City in the Age of Shakespeare*.

16. Hawkins, "Folly, Incurable Disease, and *Volpone*," argues that there is a continual interplay between what we *hear* Volpone saying, and *see* him doing, between Volpone as he wishes to perceive himself and persuade others to perceive him, and as he is in fact.

17. Edgar Schell similarly observes that "the movement of Act I is . . . the sort of movement characteristic of satire rather than comedy" (*Strangers and Pilgrims: From The Castle of Perseverance to King Lear*, 116).

center of infection, an "anti-hospital," corroding the vulnerable loves of their victims, inflating, distorting, and manipulating the disruptive self-love and self-assertion of each as a wedge to split each from the proper object of his love: Voltore from the common good (the Venetian "republic"), Corbaccio from a dutiful son, Corvino from a perfect wife.[18] In each case the point of entry is a small original flaw (small *originally,* one presumes; by the time we meet them, the game has gone on for some three years, and their cases are advanced) in the relationship. Thus, Voltore is proud of his position and eloquence for himself, not simply for their public benefit; Corbaccio's affection for his son is tainted with a grasping desire for vicarious immortality; Corvino's jealousy betrays an uneasy awareness that he is unworthy of his wife. These small private corruptions are relentlessly played upon to produce and ripen the greater public ones. The subplot provides an amusing counterchange to the main scene without disturbing its spectacular, expository character. Here we see the ludicrous aspect of what in the others turns to criminal folly, for the "flaws" of Sir Pol (parrot) and his lady concern primarily perceptual and intellectual, rather than moral, obligations. They lack self-knowledge and social sense, and their twittering stratagems result in comic humiliation and nonsense rather than pain and culpable error.[19]

Volpone seems content to extend the game indefinitely. What sets this scene in motion and brings about the crisis in their affairs that makes the drama? In one sense, the answer is obvious. The attempts upon Celia plus the entanglements with Bonario lead to the court scenes of the two final acts. One critic sees here a pattern common in Jonson's plays: folly triumphant within a limited or private space (Volpone's house), but meeting sharp correction when it tries to extend its misrule to society or the world at large.[20] But in fact, Volpone's and Mosca's forays into larger scenes of action (the mountebank scene, the two court appearances, Volpone's vexing of the gulls) are, with the exception of the final court scene (and that for a special reason), entirely successful. Correction, when it does come, comes

---

18. Alan C. Dessen sees the same process at work but identifies the cause as avarice (*Jonson's Moral Comedy,* 80). Weld observes that "All the main characters . . . are swollen with self-love and blinded by it" ("Christian Comedy: *Volpone,*" 182) and points to the relation between avarice and self-love we have already seen in *Cynthias Revels:* "[Renaissance] moralists probing the psychology of man's corruption frequently trace his love of the world to its motive, the natural (and false) self-love which leads him to try to please himself with worldly pleasures" (180).

19. See Jonas A. Barish, "The Double Plot in *Volpone.*"

20. Gabriele Bernhard Jackson, *Vision and Judgment,* 79–87; see also her "Structural Interplay in Ben Jonson's Drama."

not from without—no sharp, sane ironists, no wise, authoritative judges in this play—but from internal flaws in their own original position; flaws which their gaudy successes have previously obscured but which, as the action mounts to its proper pitch, insure that the illusion must shatter.

The fatal involvements with Celia and Bonario, both provoked by Mosca, are logical developments in the demonic project of superiority, for in them we move from the gulling of the greedy and malicious fools (Volpone: "What a rare punishment / Is avarice to it selfe?"; Mosca: "I, with our helpe, sir." [I.iv.142-43]) to the violation of the innocent.[21] Celia and Bonario have not fared well with the critics. Celia has been attacked as "too good to be true," Bonario as a self-righteous prig ("Forbear, foul ravisher") or even as a deliberate parody of melodramatic heroism.[22] Both have been criticized as artistic imperfections as well—ridiculous, ineffectual vestiges of "the ideal" in a play otherwise devoted to moral "realism." But it seems to me that such objections introduce a gratuitous confusion. In the first place, if representations of good are less "real" than those of evil, then Jonson is without a theme. For any moralist, the "ideal" is as, or more, real than prudent (actually, imprudent) vice. In the second place, Jonson has made each character's qualities clear and self-consistent, and within the moraliz-

21. Mosca tells Volpone that he has only recently learned of Celia; it may be so, but his grisly praise of Volpone's forbearance suggests the quality of imagination that will later plot Bonario's disinheritance:

>   No, sir, nor devoure
> Soft prodigalls. You shall ha' some will swallow
> A melting heire, as glibly, as your *Dutch*
> Will pills of butter, and ne're purge for't;
> Teare forth the fathers of poore families
> Out of their beds, and coffin them, alive,
> In some kind, clasping prison, where their bones
> May be forth-comming, when the flesh is rotten:
> But, your sweet nature doth abhorre these courses;
> You lothe, the widdowes, or the orphans teares
> Should wash your pavements; or their pittious cryes
> Ring in your roofes; and beate the aire, for vengeance.
>   (I.i.40-51)

This menacing, flattering account of Volpone's "pity" makes a nasty contrast to his master's relatively high-minded concerns and comparisons in the same passage.

22. Celia is more often discussed than Bonario. For a sense of the extremes, see Charles A. Hallett's reading of her as a divine presence, the only character in the play able to resist Volpone ("Jonson's Celia: A Reinterpretation of *Volpone*"; and John Creaser's description of "something in her nature [which] is both unhealthy and unconsciously self-dramatizing" (*Ben Jonson: Volpone or The Fox*, 19).

ing framework of the fiction, made them credible.[23] Why not take Jonson at his word and accept Celia as the moral equivalent of heaven, a woman perfectly loving, perfectly lovable, whose purity of intention makes her a little naive. Why not accept Bonario as "good manners," or in Platonic terms, "right opinion" to Celia's "truth." Their language and behavior are in keeping with these designations. Celia's speeches are clear and simple, even in her desperate defense against Volpone; Bonario's are thick, a little obtuse, reliable enough for ordinary business, though of course inadequate to Mosca's ironies. Despite the tincture of moral allegory, both are recognizable human characters, though of a type increasingly rare in contemporary culture and practically unknown among students of literature. There are people who remain pious, simple, and kind even into adulthood; there are people who live well on the basis of entirely conventional, unexamined notions of right and wrong.

It is in the conflict with such unimaginative characters that we begin to see the limits of the "negative capability" that Mosca brings to bear upon people and events.[24] Although he is "present to all occasions," his mastery of them remains precarious because the simple truth is always threatening to break through. Beyond his part in "exposing" and "vexing" the gulls, his main business is to separate each from his true good (as he has Volpone) by inflating self-love and self-interest to the point that they rupture the already corroded bonds of affectionate reciprocity: between Corbaccio and his son; between Corvino and his wife; between Voltore and his duty—incidentally finding time to set Sir Pol and his lady at odds. Yet these ruptured bonds release energies that severely test his powers of control. Thus we have, almost at once, the near disaster of Bonario's intervention in the rape scene and the barely adequate conspiracy that rescues the situation in the first court scene.

In the attempted rape of Celia, Volpone also gets more (and less) than he expects because Celia represents both a spiritual and a tangible good that cannot fail to rouse him, however he misunderstands or would misuse it. Here is no idle pile of gold, no sterile expectation of fantastic, never-to-be-realized pleasures. As Volpone says at the outset:

23. On Jonson's techniques of characterization, see Anne Barton, *Ben Jonson, Dramatist*, 107-8; and R. B. Parker, who notes a resemblance to "typical *commedia [dell'arte]* lovers" (*Volpone or, The Fox*, 27).

24. On Mosca's qualities, compare Stephen Greenblatt's discussion of "empathy" and "improvisation" in *Renaissance Self-Fashioning: From More to Shakespeare*, ch. 6.

> Assure thee, CELIA, he that would sell thee,
> Onely for hope of gaine, and that uncertaine,
> He would have sold his part of paradise
> For ready money, had he met a cope-man.
> (III.vii.141–44)

A hyperbolical gambit to be sure, but in it we see that even a brief exposure to Celia has moved Volpone closer to the truth. Although he misses the aptness of this condemnation for his own condition, its expression gives evidence of his developing perceptions; he sees a truth he cannot, or will not, apply. Here he rises, if only for a moment, above "CORVINO, and such earth-fed mindes, / That never tasted the true heav'n of love" (III.vii.139–40). Her "beauties miracle" has driven him beyond himself, beyond his earlier concern (expressed before his impersonation of Scoto) for maintaining his "shape," his factitious dignity. He steps, however briefly, from the order of fortune, of enchanted riches held in a perpetual potency, to a vision, however misapprehended, of the order of nature, of a real pleasure ordained for use—and for the supreme use spoken of by Celia: "a cause of life" (III.vii.136). This he quite misunderstands. He has before him the proper object of love—one embodying innocence, beauty, virtue—but does not know its proper use or end.

Still hoping to "gain no common way," he holds out to Celia what are for her the least appealing temptations: the imagined varieties of sensual indulgence that control his mind (he has still enjoyed none of them!). All he can conceive is a repetitive, sensationalist variety rather than growth, an ever more desperate pursuit (the "flying hart") of new Ovidian metamorphoses across the flickering surfaces of time and place rather than the Dantesque *vita nuova* of the emotions and spirit that love, at its best, can promise.

This episode remains spiritually unproductive in that it does not interrupt the course of Volpone's development or "damnation" but has nonetheless a signal role in the drama as a whole. It produces his most heated and eloquent speeches, exposing at once the braveness and pathos of his folly. At the moment of crisis he is content (as he realizes too late) to "play with opportunity" (264), to prefer an imagined to a real good, to cheat himself with "air," even as he and Mosca cheat Corvino and the others with "earth." Still more important is the change this episode works in Volpone, activating him, making him less dependent upon Mosca and better able to contrive his own destruction. One detects this change in the differences between his opening speech in Act I and the seduction speech to Celia. Both employ the figure of amplification, but the first (I.i.1–27) is essentially static, gradually encrusting the object of praise (his gold) with an increasingly heavy load of epithets, asides, and qualifications; while the seduction speech (III.vii. 213–39), no less full, distributes its charged masses headlong over a cleaner, firmer, more purposive syntax.[25] His interest has shifted from "being" to "doing," and this shift, though of no final benefit to him, makes possible his dramatic progress.

The first court scene, in which the "torrent is diverted upon the innocent," is a masterpiece which even Mosca concedes cannot be excelled. It represents the high-water mark of Mosca's manipulative mastery—the "rare musique" he can draw from such disparate instruments of ignorance and greed—and the apparent victory of ideas that he and Volpone have promoted throughout. There is here a double *tour de force*. The first, the harmonization of the gulls, differs only in degree from what we have already seen. Each must now be deceived in the presence of all the others; each must believe not just the particular lie that flatters his hopes, but that the common lie will serve his particular ends—a wonderful multiple self-deception. But the second part of the work, the gulling of the court, though less strikingly dramatic, is perhaps of greater thematic significance.

Up to this point the play's exposition of self-love, the primary cause and coefficient of moral evil, has been direct, if a little complex. We have been led to admire the conscious and semiconscious agents of this demonic principle and to laugh at its obvious victims. But now the play takes a paradoxical turn designed both to involve the audience more thoroughly in the spectacle and at the same time more firmly to separate the audience from the spectacle.[26] As always in Jonson, our laughter arises from the cathartic rejection and exclusion of humors—inadequate, mechanical modes of thinking, feeling, and acting—or from our sympathy with characters in the play (here, Volpone and Mosca) who perform these rejections for us. But

---

25. Beaurline observes that "Mosca's favorite linguistic device is the stupendous heap of words . . . logical subordination and a sense of orderly deduction from premises seem foreign to this style, because the main impression must be of . . . restless energy and boundless high spirits (*Jonson and Elizabethan Comedy*, 174).

26. Jonson's relation to his audience has been much commented upon. See, for example, Jonas A. Barish, "Ben Jonson and the Loathed Stage"; Peter Carlson, "Judging Spectators"; Alvin Kernan, "Shakespeare's and Jonson's View of Public Theater Audiences"; John Gordon Sweeney, "*Volpone* and the Theater of Self-Interest," and *Jonson and the Psychology of Public Theater*. These relations are more often teasing and challenging than, as Sweeney suggests, thoroughly mistrustful and antagonistic ("Theater of Self-Interest," 240)—unless, of course, the audience failed to like the play.

from this point, the moral initiative begins to shift to the audience, and we are increasingly required to judge for ourselves—a turnabout that will finally involve the rejection of Volpone and Mosca as well.

The proper question regarding the court scene is then, "What are we called upon to reject?" The stupidity and the venality of the Avocatori themselves? Of Venice? Of some stereotypically "Italian" cast of mind or institution? Of social and political judgments in general? Of any attempt to judge others and their actions? Some critics take a very superior attitude to these worthies of Venice, noting their gullibility, corruption, and severity. Yet this critical self-satisfaction seems quite unjustifiable, proceeding as it does from Jonson's pure gift to us of superior knowledge. We have *seen* what happened, and the Avocatori must *imagine* the course of events. It is precisely in this point—how we imagine evil—that Jonson proposes to catch our consciences. Moreover, any "political" line of interpretation ignores two facts about the Avocatori. Stupid and venal they may be (though efficient enough in the end), but these things are common to all courts and all judges; they have no special bearing upon the play's concerns. In addition, they do not err through stupidity or venality, nor even through a peculiar susceptibility to Voltore's fine speeches, but through that which the speeches expertly play upon, the defective moral imagination that equates evil with passion.

Voltore's "golden tongue" is often praised and first of all by Mosca himself (the sincere tribute of one craftsman to another). Yet his accomplishment, like that of any orator, lies less in "honey'd words" and "strong proofs" than in the credibility of his case. He must induce others to believe, in a doubtful situation, that his is the more probable version of motives and events. To do this, he necessarily appeals to his hearers' assumptions and experience, and since he must establish the probability of a falsehood, he also plays upon their passions and prejudices, which the audience of the play may be presumed to share.

Voltore begins by casting the whole situation in doubt (IV.v.29-59) and evokes the noncommittal response, "These be strange turns!" He redoubles the attack; the Avocatori demand "What proofes have you of this?" (93) and take testimony from the conspirators that begins to raise serious doubts: "I do begin to doubt th'imposture here" (141) and "These things, they strike, with wonder" (154). The tide turns with the appearance of Lady Pol ("These proofes are strong" [IV.vi.8]), and the reversal is completed and confirmed by the moralized spectacle of the impotent Volpone.

What has happened here? Should we accept Bonario's opinion that this is simply a court "Where multitude, and clamor overcomes" (19)? Well, yes and no. If we observe the process of the Avocatori's thinking, we see that Voltore and the others act as prompters and confirmers of an interior process of judgment, a process in which the Avocatori respond as much to the clamor within themselves as to the conspirators. As Act IV, scene v, opens we find them discussing with wondering disconcertedness the monstrous, unnatural, and unexampled tale that Celia and Bonario have set before them:

> AVOC. 1. The like of this the *Senate* never heard of.
> AVOC. 2. 'Twil come most strange to them, when we report it.
> AVOC. 4. The gentlewoman has beene ever held of un-reproved name.
> AVOC. 3. So, the young man.
> AVOC. 4. The more unnaturall part that of his father.
> AVOC. 2. More of the husband.
> AVOC. 1. I not know to give his act a name, it is so monstrous!
> AVOC. 4. But the impostor, he is a thing created t'exceed example!
> AVOC. 1. And all after times!
> AVOC. 2. I never heard a true voluptuary describ'd, but him.
>
> (IV.v.1–10)

They have accepted the story, but because it completely exceeds their experience, they can make no response to it beyond shock and wonder.

Consider in contrast their response to Voltore's conclusion:

> [VOLT.]. And, as for them [Celia and Bonario] I will conclude with this,
>   That vicious persons when they are hot, and flesh'd
>   In impious acts, their constancy abounds:
>   Damn'd deeds are done with greatest confidence.
> AVOC. 1. Take 'hem to custody, and sever them.
> AVOC. 2. 'Tis pittie, two such prodigies should live.
> AVOC. 1. Let the old gentleman be return'd, with care:
>   I'am sorry our credulitie wrong'd him.
> AVOC. 4. These are two creatures!
> AVOC. 3. I have an earthquake in me!
> AVOC. 2. Their shame (even in their cradles) fled their faces.
> AVOC. 4. You'have done a worthy service to the state, sir, in their discoverie.
> AVOC. 1. You shall heare, ere night, what punishment the court decrees upon
>   'hem.
>
> (IV.vi.50–62)

They have come to accept a story as monstrous and unnatural as the first; but while that only persuaded them, this has persuaded and *moved* them, and they express not only wonder but the mingled emotions of anger, tenderness, regret, and something deeper: "I have an earthquake in me!"

To account for this difference we may look to the key image of Voltore's peroration, "hot, and flesh'd." Our unexamined imagination of evil is just this, that it should be sensual, passionate, violent in its thrilling disruption of the common bonds of order. Yet for Jonson, as for Dante and Shakespeare, it is a central paradox of our moral nature that, while the appearance and effects of evil may be hot and violent, the cause, the essence, is deadly cold. We may remember here the frozen foundation of the *Inferno* or compare the similar treatment of the theme in *Othello,* also set in contemporary Venice. The question put to Othello is much like that put to the Avocatori: Which of two possibilities is the more credible? Which appeals better to the imagination?—that Desdemona, contrary to appearance and probability, should be hot and unfaithful or that Iago, contrary to appearance and probability, should be coolly lying? Othello entertains the latter possibility, but it does not appeal to him; his imagination cannot grasp Iago's controlled coldness.

For the first time in the play it becomes necessary (not merely possible) for us, the audience, to judge the judges. We assume a new responsibility with respect to the play and in so far as we simultaneously identify with and reject the judgments of the Avocatori, a new responsibility for the application of the satire to ourselves. It now begins to hit home. And not just for the audience, as we see in Volpone's remarkable soliloquy opening the final act:

> Well, I am here; and all this brunt is past:
> I ne're was in dislike with my disguise,
> Till this fled moment; here, 'twas good, in private,
> But, in your publike, *Cave,* whil'st I breathe.
> 'Fore god, my left legge 'gan to have the crampe;
> And I apprehended, straight, some power had strooke me
> With a dead palsey: well, I must be merry,
> And shake it off. A many of these feares
> Would put me into some villanous disease,
> Should they come thick upon me: I'le prevent 'hem.
> Give me a boule of lustie wine, to fright
> This humor from my heart; (hum, hum, hum)
> 'Tis almost gone, already: I shall conquer.
> Any device, now, of rare, ingenious knavery,
> That would possesse me with a violent laughter,
> Would make me up, againe! So, so, so, so.
> This heate is life; 'tis bloud, by this time: MOSCA!
> (V.i.)

Volpone's is a singular victory that issues in such low spirits, such violent efforts at self-assertion. But of course it has been both a victory and a defeat: success for their game, but a judgment upon Volpone. Already he begins to feel in his imagination the cramps that will be imposed upon him at the end; he unconsciously senses the moral truth that the physical sentence will only underline: one becomes what one pretends to be. Feigning impotence and affecting a demonic superiority to human limitations, he will in fact become demonic and impotent.

The scene is composed of two parts, a moment of quiet crisis and a resolve to greater violence. Both parts amplify and complete motives seen earlier. In the first place, Volpone's speech appears to be set in deliberate counterpoint to Mosca's opening of Act III:

> I feare, I shall begin to grow in love
> With my deare selfe, and my most prosp'rous parts,
> They do soe spring, and burgeon; I can feele
> A whimsey i' my bloud: (I know not how)
> Successe hath made me wanton.
>
> (III.i.1–5)

Mosca's speech expresses perfectly the principle of unfettered wit, self-love, and self-assertion he champions throughout; Volpone's reflects his nearly indelible respect for the "publike" realm—the social self, the fixed point from which, whether he will or no, the imaginary explosions of his ego are measured and confined.[27] Here he says (but does not see) what has been increasingly obvious to us, that his joint enterprise with Mosca is as unequal in its grounding as in its practice. Mosca has been expressing and enhancing his "dear selfe," his "most prosp'rous parts," while Volpone has been "disguising" and denying his own.[28] Thus, in the exchange that immediately follows, Mosca, the eager esthete, is pleased to have "gull'd the court"; Volpone, the immoral moralist, is pleased to have "diverted the torrent upon the innocent" (V.ii.16–17).

Beyond the completion of the subtly differentiated portraits of Mosca and Volpone (at last we have heard Volpone *solus*), this small scene contains a further, more decisive point, for it bears comparison not only with Mosca's soliloquy, but also with Volpone's earlier, more hectic crisis, the

---

27. See Greene, "Ben Jonson and the Centered Self," on the attraction of "centrifugal" motion.

28. Sweeney observes that Volpone and Mosca represent "two opposing aspects of theater," "self-projection" and "self-abnegation" (*Public Theater*, 77, 81), identifying the former with Volpone and the latter with Mosca. This is their announced program, but the results are quite the reverse.

"interview" with Celia. That crisis provides Volpone's first failure, his misprision of the nature of love, his imaginative attempt to exhaust its effects without ever discovering its purpose. But his failure here is more intimate and more important. If romantic love has, as Celia asserts, "ever been a cause of life," the social shame, the judgment Volpone now experiences has often been the cause of something equally important—self-knowledge and self-correction. Whatever may be the state of Volpone's vital energies, his capacity for folly is undiminished, and he here proves able to ignore the insights available from self-disgust, even as he earlier misused his admiration for Celia. His "disease" is a sign of potential health, but as in any disease the crisis leads either to recovery or death. Volpone chooses death, albeit a death disguised as recovery.

The "violent laughter" he now begins to pursue represents at once a spiritual suicide and his final failure as a lover—he fails to love himself.[29] Volpone himself makes the first point: "To make a snare, for mine owne necke! and run / My head into it wilfully! with laughter!" (V.xi.1-2). Indeed, he now performs a series of self-exhausting, suicidal "vexings" that have no end in view, much on the pattern of the wandering, sterile pleasure proposed to Celia.[30] But for the second point, we need to recall the special character of Jonsonian laughter. Like all laughter, it signals a relief that arises from some crucial union or separation. But the laughter of union, of lovers, generations, societies, perceptions reunited after dangerous division is seldom heard in Jonson. Much more frequent is the laughter of separation, the relief accompanying the splitting of things improperly or unnaturally conjoined: folly and dignity, selfishness and power, error and truth. Volpone's "violent laughter" is a perversion of this bracing, ironic laughter of separation that is analogous to his earlier perversion of the pastoral mode. He uses laughter to separate things which do in fact belong together—himself and other men—and to enforce the sterile illusion of his superiority to them. In doing so, he denies his nature and fails to properly know or care for himself. In willing his own social degradation, he boldly cuts the last thread that had bound him to other men and to his own better nature.

Mosca, however, is at the same time developing in the opposite direc-

---

29. Alexander Leggatt has discussed "The Suicide of Volpone" as a victory for Volpone as artist and performer.

30. Robert N. Watson describes Volpone as "a man searching for a satisfactory role in which to cast himself" (*Ben Jonson's Parodic Strategy: Literary Imperialism in the Comedies*, 86).

tion. He proves to be not quite devil enough. The ironic reserve breaks down, and the master tempter falls prey to the illusion with which he had cheated all the others (including Volpone), the illusion that he alone can possess the fullness of things. Critics have been sufficiently troubled by this change in Mosca to sniff out "preparations" for it early in the play. But the search for such preparations is, I think, both illusory and unnecessary.[31] It is illusory because Mosca's "possession" in Act V results from his opportune exploitation of Volpone's unforeseen initiative, which itself grows out of the unforeseen (and unforeseeable) frustrations and complications attending the botched rape of Celia. (We may well imagine that Mosca has been ready for some such trick, but hardly that he planned it.) It is unnecessary because Mosca's change is less to be understood as an inevitable consequence of what comes before than as an unexpected psychological and artistic masterstroke of Jonson's. Without it, Mosca the compleat parasite and Mosca the demonic tempter would soar off into the allegorical sublime in the company of Ariel and Mephistopheles, to the evident impoverishment of the play. For it is essential to Jonson's vision and purpose that all elements should become subject to a final judgment in a common court, under a common law.

The final scene, which actually encompasses V.x-xii, begins with a question that could serve as an epigraph to a study of Jonsonian comedy: "Are all the parties here?" The scene is typical—Jonson frequently ends his plays with judgment scenes, formal or virtual[32]—and the question goes to the heart of the matter. Like all comic artists, Jonson has for his largest subject wholeness and particularity: the wholeness of societies, families, persons; and the particularities of interests, desires, and self-conceptions, which either prevent wholeness, or in the right circumstances with the right direction may be made to contribute to it. But unlike most comic physicians (most of his predecessors and contemporaries, that is; in this, he is quite the modern), he presents an allopathic comedy for his patient audience. In the mature comedies we see little reconciliation within or between characters. This play also moves away from reconciliation, separating and exposing the plotters and assigning them their several punishments. What wholeness exists is only in the judging mind that deals equally, that is, appropriately,

---

31. Parker notes the play's "sense of spontaneity—of farcical improvisation and repetition, parody, and balance, rather than causality" (*Volpone or, The Fox*, 28-29).

32. Katharine Eisaman Maus observes, "In Jonsonian drama, the trial at its most effective becomes the recognition scene that makes the truth manifest and civilized community possible" (*Ben Jonson and the Roman Frame of Mind*, 127).

with all concerned. Yet this wholeness of judgment depends upon the greater particularization of the things it judges. Each must be separated cleanly, surgically from the tissue of circumstances to be seen for what it is. Therefore, "Are all the parties here?" Parts they must remain (no Shakespearean integrations here; this is failed romance, frustrated consummation), yet each must be present and accounted for.

The business of judging belongs, of course, to the audience; the Avocatori merely perform the sentencing.[33] And for the audience only three characters remain to be judged, Corbaccio and Corvino having been sufficiently humiliated in the first court scene, Sir Pol having been exposed shortly before (V.iv). Voltore, the last and most considerable of the gulls, is also humiliated upon the very point by which he had triumphed: his public capacity as orator and advocate. So too Mosca, who comes short in what had been his strength. The former master of all occasions here fails to understand the situation, fails to "come to composition" when he has the chance:

> MOS.   (Wil you gi' me halfe?
> VOLP.   First, I'le be hang'd.
> MOS.   I know,
>   Your voice is good, cry not so lowd)
> AVO. I.   Demand
>   The Advocate. Sir, did you not affirme,
>   VOLPONE was alive?
> VOLP.   Yes, and he is;
>   This gent'man told me so, (thou shalt have halfe.)
> MOS.   Whose drunkard is this same? speake some, that know him:
>   I never saw his face. (I cannot now
>   Affoord it you so cheape.
> VOLP.   No?)
>   (V.xii.63-70)

As with the others, Mosca's greed to have all loses all.

Volpone's case is the most difficult, for his has been the noblest error. Like that of Narcissus, his damnation results from the misdirection of

---

33. The Avocatori are often faulted for the harshness of the sentences, but Jonson could have cited the authority of Contarini: "Alwaies the Advocators doe propounde that punishment, which to that sorte of offence doth seeme most sharp and grievous, their office and dutie being more to incline to severity than to mercie" (*The Commonwealth and Government of Venice*, 91). Jonson appears to depart from Contarini in making the Avocatori the final judges in the case; see Daniel C. Boughner, "Lewkenor and *Volpone*."

impulses and capacities originally good. We have seen him mistake or abuse his situation, his motives, Celia, and his public identity, but one final, annihilating exposure remains: Mosca's betrayal of his affection. In the scene preceding (V.xi), he discovers that Mosca has driven out the grotesques and locked the house, but he still hopes for the best: "His meaning may be truer than my fears." Even in the final scene, after explaining the situation to Mosca ("I was a'most lost") and being rejected as a "busie knave," appealing to him by name ("Mosca!") and hearing only "Whom I intend to bury, like a gentleman," Volpone retains enough distance for the wry comment, "I, quicke, and cosen me of all" (52–60). But at the last there can be no further mistake, and his final, inarticulate appeal comes with an awful nakedness:

> MOS.   Most grave fathers,
> If such an insolence, as this, must passe
> Upon me, I am silent: 'twas not this,
> For which you sent, I hope.
> AVO. 2.   Take him away.
> (VOLP. MOSCA.)
> AVO. 3.   Let him be whipt.
> (VOLP.   Wilt thou betray me?
> Cosen me?)
>
>   (74–79)

For all the attempted ironic, Satanic self-sufficiency, one point of human vulnerability remained, a point of friendship or fellowship in which he imagined himself still joined. Now he must see—and feel—that he is, and has been, alone.[34]

This brief moment of pathos—and it is only a moment—comes unexpectedly and is not strictly necessary since any little puff could bring down the house of plot and counterplot at this point. Yet to do it in this way creates an effect that Jonson, his preface notwithstanding, might be hard put to defend in terms of "comic law," for it redeems our sympathy for Volpone precisely at the point we are called upon to reject him.[35] That the ending should contain neither marriages nor rejoicing poses, as Jonson claims, no serious difficulty. But that, into the strict arena of comic justice

---

34. Cf. William Empson's comments on Volpone's need for Mosca's love and friendship as that of "a criminal for his accomplice" ("Volpone," 664–65).

35. We may recall that Shakespeare's tragic heroes often recover their dignity just before the end. See Russ McDonald, "Sceptical Visions: Shakespeare's Tragedies and Jonson's Comedies."

he has been at such pains to construct, he should introduce our compassion for the pain of the chief sinner is perhaps more than this comic form can be expected to bear. We may be sure, however, that this violation of form is fully intended. It leaves us with a final impression of Volpone not only as Protean "voluptuary" or "impostor" or "suicidal" ironist, but also as failed and disappointed "lover," the narcissistic "famisht mind" and "flying hart" disappointed at last even in the one concession to nature's demands. Bacon observes in "Of Friendship," that even such emperors as Julius, Augustus, and Tiberius Caesar, "men so wise, of such strength and severity of mind, and so extreme lovers of themselves . . . found their own felicity (though as great as ever happened to mortal men) but as an half piece, except they mought have a friend to make it entire." And, Bacon concludes, "if [a man] have not a friend, he may quit the stage."[36]

* * *

We saw that in *Cynthias Revels* there are two sensibilities, two strategies, almost two artists at work: the poetic, Platonizing moralist who writes of Echo and Narcissus, Cynthia and Arete; and the satirist of manners who "discovers" and presents to us all the witty inanities of self-love in a courtly setting. The mediating link between these sensibilities, Crites is scholar and observer, judge both of what is done and ought to be done and therefore, maker of the integrating masque.[37] All this is clever and correct enough, but too mechanical to maintain a lively sense of drama.

In *Volpone* the essential materials are not much changed, but their interrelations have become more complex and coherent. Incident and character, while not so verisimilar as in a history play or tragedy (*Sejanus*, for example), have the verisimilitude appropriate to comedy rather than comic allegory. Most striking is the close interweaving of materials, tragic and satiric, the morality play and the city comedy. As in *Cynthias Revels,* Jonson has two plays in potential: "the damnation of Volpone" and a satire on avarice, "the gulling of the greedy." But here these elements are so tightly pulled together that they not only support but mutually impel each other. Each of the gulls suffers a small, understated damnation or annihilating judgment, while Mosca and Volpone, the great deceivers-would-be, are themselves finally (self-)gulled. Each set of characters becomes the agent of the other's undoing. Volpone and Mosca congratulate themselves, rightly,

---

36. Francis Bacon, "Of Friendship," in Spedding, *Works*, 6:439, 443.
37. On the character of Crites, see Wyman H. Herendeen, "'Like a Circle Bounded in Itself': Jonson, Camden, and the Strategies of Praise," 162–67.

on assisting in the punishment of avarice, while the gulls provide the stimulus and the opportunity for the ironists to overreach and destroy themselves. The two moods contrast with and complement each other, acting and reacting with increasing speed and intimacy until the final arrest, the final restraining judgment, which does not resolve (what could?) these explosive materials of human folly but does disperse and restrict them for a moment.

At the same time, Jonson succeeds in involving the audience more fully. He refuses to locate a controlling ideal within the play, supplying only a vision (Celia) and a reminder (Bonario) of the good, but for the most part letting passion run its sinuous, deadly course. He realizes the greater dramatic potential of evil, the exhilaration of the downward spiral it traces. The good, as he sees it, is far less promising dramatically, because its operation consists of discrete, discontinuous, incremental stances, judgments, and corrections. Passion proposes briefly; judgment disposes at length. Judgment may be the bit to control ill deeds and the spur to promote good ones, but it can never equal in dramatic interest the passionate horse itself. Jonson's solution to this fundamental artistic problem is to leave whatever controlling morality is possible to the audience, drawing them into the battle between vice and virtue in a new way.

The synthesis of materials in *Volpone* represents the best strategy and the finest actual embodiment of the negative elements of Jonson's moral vision. His theme is ever narcissistic self-love; its operations within the personality, driving one to isolation and despair; and its correlative operations outside the self, breaking the bonds of affection and obligation that hold together a marriage, a family, a commonwealth. In this play better than in any other, these are shown to cohere, to imply each other in ways that, working separately, neither the psychological moralist nor the social critic could so fully demonstrate. In addition, he has given the audience a new role in the presentation and understanding of the drama, for it is now the spectator who must act the part of the controlling ego that perceives the dangers and works out, however fitfully, a healthy way of loving and living.[38]

38. Schell observes that there remains a "gap between the comic and satiric structures of *Volpone* [which] calls for an act of faith on the part of both its creator and its audience, for both must believe for the duration of the play that avarice is its own punishment without being able to make that probable in the affairs of men" (*Strangers and Pilgrims,* 149).

Chapter III

Epic and Epigram

*I*n Jonson's carefully arranged *Workes* of 1616, the *Epigrammes* appear between the plays and the masques, and this placement reflects their central and transitional significance.¹ Much they share with the plays: here too are alchemists, bawds, whores, gamesters (reformed and otherwise), lechers, surly captains, shifty lieutenants, spies, effete courtiers, corrupt lawyers, self-important statesmen would-be, preening poetasters, ignorant critics—the whole "wise world," as Mosca calls it, of "Parasites, or Sub-Parasites" (*Volpone,* III.i.12–13). But they share also in the higher world of the masques: Here too are the king and his true courtiers, wise judges, brave soldiers and men of affairs, generous patrons and patronesses. And beyond the politically and socially prominent, we find a crucial middle class, including Jonson's own teacher, friends, fellow actors, poets, scholars, children—and not least of all, Jonson himself, whose personality and presence dominate this collection even more thoroughly than Volpone dominates his play. We have here a portrait of Jonson's whole world, literary and practical, a common ground on which all the elements of his experience come together and interact in a way unique among his works and, with the partial exception of Montaigne's *Essais,* unique in the works of his time.² Jonson himself describes them in the dedication as "the

---

1. Stephen Orgel observes that we find in the nondramatic poetry those who, "steadfast in a world of vice, misrule, and decay . . . provide the links between the ideal vision of the Jonsonian masque and the satiric vision of Jonsonian drama" (*The Jonsonian Masque*, 194).
2. On the "presence" of Jonson in the book, both as speaker and poet, see Edward Partridge's seminal article "Jonson's *Epigrammes*: The Named and the Nameless" and the discussion by Claude J. Summers and Ted-Larry Pebworth in *Ben Jonson*, 138–57. Annabel Patterson has made a similar argument regarding the *Under-wood*, calling it a "retrospective of his career, a retelling of his relations with the state, the stage, friends, patrons, politicians [in which] Jonson's self is also present" ("Lyric and Society," 153); see also her *Censorship*

ripest of my studies." This statement is invariably reproduced by critics, though it would be hard to say whether more in wonder, or derision, or simply because it's there. I hope to show that Jonson is here, as often, his own best (though not most explicit) critic and that his description of these poems should still command our attention and respect.

It is necessary first of all to clear away some of the underbrush of misconceived criticism that has, while always valuing some of the epigrams, caused neglect of the collection as a whole. The earliest of Jonson's modern readers approached his work with narrow preconceptions regarding the nature of poetry. Swinburne quotes Sir Walter Scott's objection to Jonson's "using the language of scavengers and nightmen." Herford and Simpson repeatedly regret Jonson's deficient "lyricism," his "inability to sing," and congratulate him whenever he "breaks into song." While admiring the tenderness of the elegies and epitaphs, the nobility of Jonson's praise of worthy friends, and the easy familiarity of "Inviting a Friend to Supper," they characterize the collection as a "commonly pedestrian and too often malodorous wilderness."[3]

More recently, the appreciation of Jonson's poems has suffered from a similarly narrow idea of the poet's proper tone and stance. We seem increasingly to require that poets be not only conscious and critical (which Jonson always is), but also self-conscious and self-critical to the point of self-mistrust (which Jonson seldom is). This has led to some peculiar inversions in our understanding of particular poems. Poems once praised for their mastery of complex experiences are now praised for their confessions of inadequacy to these same experiences. Thus, "On My First Sonne" (*Epigrammes,* XLV) is commended for refusing consolation, and "To Heaven" (*Forrest,* XV) for its frank inability to worship in a satisfactory way.[4] Some have also wished to reject the "arrogant" or "authoritarian" Jonson, the *censor morum* who speaks frequently in the *Epigrammes*.[5] Such a rejection fails to appreciate the essential "control and economy" that may make the epigrammatist "seem brusque, cold, uncompromising, authoritative, 'authoritarian'";[6] and it fails to sufficiently distinguish between the

---

and Interpretation: The Conditions of Writing and Reading in Early Modern England, 121–44.

3. Swinburne, *A Study of Ben Jonson,* 95–96. H&S, 2:337–413; for the *Epigrammes* in particular, 2:342–68.

4. See Judith Kegan Gardiner, *Craftsmanship in Context: The Development of Ben Jonson's Poetry,* 44–51; and William Kerrigan, "Ben Jonson Full of Shame and Scorn."

5. Gardiner's discussion of the *Epigrammes* (*Craftsmanship in Context,* 12–53) is typical of this tendency: she regards them as "less mature" than the later poetry.

6. Barbara Herrnstein Smith, *Poetic Closure: A Study of How Poems End,* 208–9.

"moralist" and the "moralizer." The "moralizer" pretends to an authority derived from his own spurious purity; the "moralist" relies upon his own intimate experience of the temptations and vices he condemns and warns against. As Jonson remarks in *The Forrest,* "Next, to that vertue [innocence], is to know vice well, / And her blacke spight expell" (XI.3-4). Jonson's capacity for arrogance is well known, but in the *Epigrammes* the speaker's close involvement with the objects of his criticism and his own self-criticism, make him more moralist than moralizer; Ben Jonson's personal shortcomings are only raw material for the achieved speaker, the "Jonson," visible in the poems.

But the greatest hindrance to our appreciation has been the problem of form. Although particular beauties have often been admired and anthologized, no one, until quite recently, has known what to do with this various collection of elegant compliment, tender epitaph, witty satire, and brutal, scatological invective. Many have implicitly agreed with the Oxford editors who, throwing up their hands, declared it a "quite unmanageable wilderness of verse-kinds."[7] The result has been that much criticism of the nondramatic poetry, however acute, has been couched in topical analyses and arguments that pay little or no attention to Jonson's shaping purpose in such collections as the *Epigrammes* and *The Forrest.*

The best recent criticism of the *Epigrammes* has begun to find ways to manage this "wilderness," conceding the evident diversity, while searching for unifying rhythms of intention or form. Jean Humez and others have found a loose overall structure with antecedents in classical satire, comparable to the antimasque/masque movement apparent in many of Jonson's works. Bruce Smith has tried to confine the multiplicity to a few broad categories of competing form—theater, portrait gallery, commonwealth—which, he argues, finally complement and reinforce each other. Edward Partridge's study, mostly devoted to the theme of "names" and "naming" first analyzed by David Wykes but also containing valuable observations on the uses of juxtaposition, rhetorical intimacy and distance, and other topics, is the richest and most suggestive so far.[8]

7. H&S, 2:341.
8. Jean McMahon Humez, "The Manners of Epigram: A Study of the Epigram Volumes of Martial, Harington, and Jonson," Ph.D. diss.; Bruce R. Smith, "Ben Jonson's *Epigrammes*: Portrait-Gallery, Theater, Commonwealth"; David Wykes, "Ben Jonson's 'Chaste Booke': The *Epigrammes.*" See also the judicious discussion by Sara J. van den Berg in *The Action of Ben Jonson's Poetry*, ch. 4.
Other recent studies include R. V. Young, Jr., "Style and Structure in Jonson's *Epigrammes*"; Ira Clark, "Ben Jonson's Imitation"; Jack D. Winner, "Ben Jonson's *Epigrammes* and the Conventions of Formal Verse Satire"; Jonathan Z. Kamholtz, "Ben Jonson's *Epi-*

Useful as these and others are, several considerations point to the possibility of a more inclusive and compelling account of the book's unity than has previously been attempted. The first is Jonson's known character as an artist. All of his mature work employs a similar method: seizing upon a central theme, symbol, or purpose, and using it as a magnet to attract and organize the iron filings of observations, incident, and character.[9] Much of the composition (and the entire arrangement) of the *Epigrammes* dates from the same period (1605–1612) as the major plays. It is unlikely that this characteristic centralizing intensity of vision and method plays no part in such poetic collections as the *Epigrammes*. It is more unlikely still when we consider that in the *Workes* the *Epigrammes* challenge comparison with the best of the plays by virtue of their climactic position (following *Catiline* and preceding the masques), their elaborate dedication to Pembroke, Jonson's most important patron (*Catiline* is also dedicated to him; he alone is twice so honored), and the remarkable claim already noted that they are "the ripest of my studies."

In the following discussion, I will intertwine three related propositions concerning the *Epigrammes*. First, that the "booke" possesses unities of purpose and effect deriving from the manipulation of the omnipresent speaker, "Jonson," and the use of fundamental and recurrent metaphors: two encompassing the whole (the procession, the battle) and two distributed throughout (the body and its shifting passions, contract and payment). Second, that the purpose and effect are best described as "epic" or "heroic" and thus go considerably beyond Martial, the immediate model. Third, that the "booke" functions (and was intended to function) within the Jonson canon as a response to the problems of self-love posed in the plays generally and in *Volpone* quintessentially.

※ ※ ※

I To the Reader
Pray thee, take care, that tak'st my booke in hand,
To reade it well: that is, to understand.

What is more piercing than simplicity? None of the armed prologues,

---

grammes and Poetic Occasions"; Jennifer Brady, "'Beware the Poet': Authority and Judgment in Jonson's *Epigrammes*." See also the introduction to Richard Dutton's edition, *Ben Jonson: Epigrams and The Forest*.

9. See Heffner, "Unifying Symbols."

epilogues, inductions, and interludes with which the plays are so liberally festooned confronts us so directly as this little rhyme. In those, we resist or succumb to the force of boisterous argument; here the challenge is quieter and perhaps less easily met.[10]

How should we read a book of epigrams? What kind of "book" is it? The earliest (Hellenistic) collections of epigrams were likely arranged on the principle of *variatio*. And Martial, traditionally acknowledged as the first to collect epigrams into books, seems also to have cultivated an appearance of deliberate carelessness in their arrangement.[11] Judging from his comments and practice in his first twelve books, he seems mainly concerned that they be neither too long nor too monotonous. Thus he limits his *libellus* to about one hundred poems and carefully varies them in subject, tone, and rhetorical technique. Some of the books are furnished with special introductory or concluding poems addressing the emperor, the publisher, particular friends or rivals, or commenting playfully on the relation between author and reader. The first book ends, for example, with

> Cui legisse satis non est epigrammata centum
> nil illi satis est, Caeciliane, mali.
>
> (1.118)

(He who is not glutted with the reading of a hundred epigrams is not glutted, Cecilianus, with any amount of badness.)[12]

In other books, he does not even trouble to mark beginnings and ends; whatever unity they may possess is rhetorical, not formal.

As has often been noticed, Jonson borrows many of Martial's book-making techniques, especially from Martial's comparatively elaborate and

---

10. On this poem, see Ilona Bell, "Circular Strategies and Structures in Jonson and Herbert."

11. Matthew S. Santirocco, *Unity and Design in Horace's Odes*, ch. 1. See also Ann Baynes Coiro, *Robert Herrick's Hesperides and the Epigram Book Tradition*, ch. 3. *The Greek Anthology*, the earliest parts of which antedate Martial by a century or more, is arranged in books according to subject. But this arrangement dates only from the 10th–12th century A.D.; the earliest fragments were in the alphabetical order of the first letters of the poems. See W. R. Paton's introduction to the Loeb edition, vii-viii.

12. All quotations and translations are from the Loeb edition of the *Epigrams*. Although none of Martial's first twelve books contains precisely one hundred poems (and no two contain the same number), the average for all the books is close to one hundred. Jonson's total of 133 poems exceeds Martial's longest (118). See Gordon Braden, *The Classics and English Renaissance Poetry*, 180–96.

self-conscious first book.[13] Thus we begin in both cases with an explanatory preface or dedication, followed by opening addresses to the reader, to the book, to or about the bookseller, and to the emperor or king. Both include gibes at critics, fops and other social grotesques, compliments to the king, nobility, patrons and fellow poets. Both adopt the stance of the knowing man about town, court, and country, who freely distributes praise or blame upon whatever catches his eye, and range in subject from high to low, from delicate epitaph to brutal scatology. But in analyzing Jonson's claim that he is restoring "the old way, and the true" (*Epigrammes,* XVIII) in the writing of epigrams, we may identify three less obvious elements in Martial that Jonson found important enough to imitate and adapt to his own needs.

Both poets defend the seriousness and dignity of the epigram and praise the things it does best—observing, manifesting, and judging manners and men—over against such supposedly higher forms of poetry as tragedy and the heroic or romantic epic. Martial, replying to those who call epigrams "frivolous" (*lusus*), asserts that the tragedians are more frivolous than he. Why? Because while men may praise tragedies, they *read* epigrams (4.49). Addressing those whose favorite reading features the adventures and "monsters" of epic fable, he remarks

> hoc lege, quod possit dicere vita "Meum est."
> non hic Centaures, non Gorgonas Harpyiasque
>   invenies: hominem pagina nostra sapit.
> sed non vis, Mamurra, tuos cognoscere mores
>   nec te scire. . . .
>
>   (10.4.8–12)

(Read this of which Life can say: "'Tis my own." Not here will you find Centaurs, not Gorgons and Harpies: 'tis of man my page smacks. But you do not wish, Mamurra, to recognize your own manners, or to know yourself.)

These issues, expressed in much the same terms, are already familiar to a reader of Jonson's Folio prologue to *Every Man in His Humour,* where the "deeds and language, such as men doe use" (21) stand in opposition to the parodied extravagances of contemporary adventure and romance. Similarly, in the dedication to the *Epigrammes,* we find the heedless readers, like Mamurra, who have "so much love to their diseases, as they would rather

---

13. On Jonson and the significance of "books," see Richard C. Newton, "Jonson and the (Re-)Invention of the Book."

make a partie for them, than be either rid, or told of them" (ll. 13–15). In both poets, epigrams are seen to challenge comparison with the generally acknowledged higher forms, such as epic and tragedy, in bringing us to self-knowledge and self-control.

The second point in which Jonson imitates, even exceeds, Martial is the prominence he gives to the character of the poet or speaker. For all the memorable lines in Martial's twelve books, the personality of the speaker predominates—his wit, humor, reverence (and more frequent irreverence), his capacity for friendship, his love of the countryside, his amusement at or ferocious condemnation of vice, folly, and pretense. This personality is the conspicuous agent of the serious (though playfully fulfilled) purpose of self-knowledge and self-control, embodying the theme of the work, presenting the fully developed response of a civilized man, Marcus Valerius Martialis, to the civilization in which he finds himself, and we are charmed, rather than persuaded, to adopt his view of things. Characteristic differences in tone and purpose between the speakers of Martial's and of Jonson's epigrams have often been noted, Martial's displaying a "curious ambivalence . . . a suggestion that he in part relishes the grotesquery, corruption, and lubriciousness of a disintegrating society"; while Jonson's reveals "beneath the reserved surface, the pressure of the mastered emotion, the guarded vulnerability . . . that distinguishes [him] from Martial, who is both more brilliant and more brutal."[14] Indeed, Jonson's speaker is "heavier" than Martial's, as willing to use a sledgehammer as a scalpel and obliged to reject or embrace the "deeds" and "men" he encounters, rather than content himself with merely knowing or exposing them. He is more "heavily" involved because it is *his* world represented here, not simply "Rome" or "London," but all the significant points of reference in the poet's life and affairs, and he bears a special responsibility to see, to speak, and to act, that he may preserve and further its civility.

The third and most significant area of Jonson's imitation of Martial concerns what the speaker does. In both cases, powers of observation and comment are crucial. The speaker must see the object clearly and completely, and must present in the poem both what it is and what it means. Hence the emphasis on seeing in Martial (his speaker must often penetrate deceptive appearances, connect disparate impressions to find a pattern, or make finer distinctions than others had or could) and on the still more

---

14. R. V. Young, Jr., "Jonson, Crashaw, and the Development of the English Epigram," 139. Smith, *Poetic Closure*, 209.

synthetic (involving both seeing and speaking) activity of "naming" in Jonson. The Jonsonian speaker presents himself explicitly as a maker or revealer of names (*Epigrammes* X, XXX, LXXVI, LXXVII, CII, CXV, CXXVIII), and comparison with the *locus classicus* in Plato's *Cratylus* indicates the scope of Jonson's enterprise.[15] In the *Cratylus,* Socrates confronts two interlocutors, one convinced that names are merely random sounds associated with objects by convention, the other maintaining, rather vaguely, that there is some "true" connection between names and things. Socrates' attitude to this reported dispute is provocative and playful, exposing the apparent weaknesses and possible absurdities latent in either extreme position and leaving the reader to find what middle ground he can. Along the way, however, he introduces several important ideas about "name-giving" and the "name-giver" (388–90).[16] In the first place, he argues that names should be regarded as an "instrument" (*organon*) to "teach one another something, and separate things according to their natures," the name being "an instrument of teaching and of separating reality, as a shuttle is an instrument of separating the web" (388A-C). The coordinate activities of "separating" and "teaching" are homologous to the "observation" and "comment" of the epigrammatist. Moreover, few men are capable of "making names":

> Socrates: Then it is not for every man, Hermogenes, to give names, but for him who may be called the name-maker [*onomatourgos*]; and he, it appears, is the lawgiver [*nomothetes*], who is of all the artisans among men the rarest. (389A)

That the work of the name-maker be well done requires two further stipulations. First, as "lawgiver" he must work closely with or be "supervised by" the "dialectician," "the man who knows how to ask and answer questions" (390D). Second, as Socrates explains,

> must not the lawgiver also know how to embody in the sounds and syllables that name which is fitted by nature for each object? Must he not make and give all his names with his eye fixed upon the absolute or ideal name, if he is to be an authoritative giver of names? (389D)

This is Jonson's territory. Epigrams are the most "dialectical" of nondramatic forms, and the epigrammatist must ask and answer questions, test objects, test names, and test the fitness of names to objects on every page,

---

15. On Jonson's familiarity with the *Cratylus* and the significance of "naming" throughout his work, see Barton, *Ben Jonson, Dramatist,* 170–93.

16. All quotations and translations are from the Loeb edition, *Plato,* vol. 6.

and almost in every poem. And for Jonson, more than Martial, it is essential that his name-giving be recognized by competent critics as "authoritative" and derive its authority from some ideal "name," associated for his present purpose with the dedicatee, William, Earl of Pembroke, whose name provides "an epigramme, on all man-kind" (CII). Edward Partridge has stressed the central importance of "naming" in the epigrams, seeing it as the poet's habitual activity which creates a named circle of admiration, sympathy, obligation, and common effort, while excluding a nameless horde of beasts and frauds.[17] But as the discussion in the *Cratylus* indicates, the point can be pressed further. For the name-giver "separates" reality not only in a moral or social sense, but in a more fundamental way, not merely assigning objects to categories, but discovering and describing the properties of the categories themselves. Like the physicist, whose increasing vocabulary of names (mus, pi-mesons, quarks) do not so much "describe" reality as *constitute* a particular kind of reality as a field for investigation and understanding, the Jonsonian epigrammatist (poet, not herald) not only separates the moral sheep from the immoral goats, but also stimulates our consideration of what we mean by the names we think with, such names as "virtue" and "vice" or the two most frequent "names" in the collection, "good" and "great."[18] What content and connection do they have and should they have? To the extent that the poet succeeds in this sort of naming, he defines the moral field, showing us not only how to act, but how to think and feel about moral categories.[19]

Thus, in several ways Jonson reshapes or gives different weight to elements found in Martial. The clearest mark of their overall difference

---

17. Partridge, "Jonson's *Epigrammes*." Partridge's argument that Jonson's aim is to create "one great society of the noble living and the noble dead" (198) has been attacked by Don E. Wayne ("Poetry and Power in Ben Jonson's *Epigrammes*: The Naming of Facts or the Figuring of Social Relations?"). Wayne sees in the *Epigrammes* a society "hardly different in structure from the unnatural society depicted in *Volpone*" (86), in which Jonson's pervasive irony lays bare "the paranoid basis of all relationships, even those of love and friendship, in a world where one's virtue or one's art is one's property" (93). This is an instructive misreading; the Hobbesian "individualism" Wayne describes is present—but as the problem to be overcome, not the final vision.

18. See Michael James Preston, "A Verse Concordance to the Non-dramatic Poetry of Ben Jonson," Ph.D. diss., 1620-24. "Great" appears 45 times; "good," 29.

19. Cf. Kathleen Williams' observation that, in the heroic poetry of Spenser and Milton, "we . . . are to learn not so much a set of facts as how to form a set of values. . . . it teaches us understanding, the power to see clearly, to make distinctions between matters not readily distinguished, to choose, or, in [a] characteristically Miltonic phrase, to see and know, and so to act" ("Milton, Greatest Spenserian," 30).

appears in the fundamental metaphors each chooses to describe the central "action" in the "theater" of his epigrams. Martial's scene is the Roman festival of the Floralia. As he states in the "Epistle" prefaced to his first book,

> epigrammata illis scribuntur qui solent spectare Florales.
> non intret Cato theatrum meum aut, si intraverit, spectet.
> videor mihi meo iure facturus si epistulam versibus clusero:
>   Nosses iocosae dulce cum sacrum Florae
>   festosque lusus et licentiam volgi,
>   cur in theatrum, Cato severe, venisti?
>   an ideo tantum veneras, ut exires?

(Epigrams are written for those who are accustomed to look on the Games of Flora. Let no Cato enter my theatre, or if he enters, let him look on. I think I may justifiably close my epistle in verse:

> You knew the rites to jocund Flora dear,
> The testive quips and license of the rout;
> Why on our scene, stern Cato, enter here?
> Did you then enter only to go out?)

Similarly in 1.35, defending himself against the objections of a friend who does not see the need for licentiousness in his verses, he exclaims,

> quis Floralia vestit et stolatum
> permittet meretricibus pudorem?
> lex haec carminibus dataest iocosis,
> ne possint, nis pruriant, iuvare.
>   (8–11)

(Who brings garments into Flora's festival, and permits prostitutes the modesty of the stole? This is the rule assigned to jocular poems, to be unable to please unless they are prurient.)

The Floralia was a fertility festival, and like most such rituals, it attempted to assure the continued vitality of individuals and social groups by breaking through what are seen to be the artificial restraints of ordinary social life to reach the richer, darker, more passionate, more natural substrata.[20] Like spectators at the Games of Flora, the reader of Martial must be ready for

---

20. Franz Altheim observes of the Floralia that "one special feature deserves notice; . . . the courtesans appeared in public. They carried out sham fights . . . and, above all, stripped themselves and gave vent to all manner of indecent gestures and speeches" (*A History of Roman Religion*, 122). See also Ovid, *Fasti*, 5.183 ff., and Tacitus, *Annals*, 2.49.

anything, ready to encounter in every poem, in every literary game, dangerous and vital things unsuspected, obscured, or kept at bay by the "clothing" of custom. His reward will be a heightened, enlivening perception of things as they are, not as they seem. That the games are licentious or "immoral" is exactly the point. The ordinary rules of moral accountability must be suspended: man, free of the necessity to act, shall godlike see.

Jonson, however, is a more ambitious poet than Martial. Some of the licentiousness of the Floralia he has adopted, it being similar in its energies to the "stripping and whipping" of contemporary satire; but it seldom amounts to much, having been subsumed to a greater purpose. Jonson calls attention to the difference when he announces in the dedication that "in my Theater . . . Cato, if he liv'd, might enter without scandall." Here moral considerations will not be suspended. To the contrary, in addressing Pembroke he introduces fundamental metaphors—the procession and the battle—which, like the Floralia, indicate extraordinary moments of ritual or ceremonial significance. Unlike the Floralia, however, these involve not the suspension, but the clarification, celebration, and defense of social values.[21] Thus, in the dedication Pembroke is offered "the honor of leading forth so many good, and great names (as my verses mention on the better part) to their remembrance with posteritie." In the epigram addressed to him (CII), he appears as the central figure "in this strife / Of vice, and vertue; wherein all great life / Almost, is exercis'd" (5-7), the one whom "they, that hope to see / "The common-wealth still safe, must studie" (19-20). The two metaphors complement each other and point up the chief differences with Martial. There is "strife" in Martial, not only in the sham fights and hunts of the Floralia itself, but in the continual challenge to poet and reader adequately to meet all comers. In Jonson this literary and perceptual *agon* remains and is even further amplified by the seesawing "battle" for predominance within the book waged by the virtuous named and the vicious nameless, but it is finally ancillary to an appreciation of the moral struggle in the lives of the speaker and those he speaks of, and to the implications of that struggle for the "common-wealth" of civilized life. In Martial we find

---

21. Jonson's intentions have been interpreted by Stanley Fish as "negative and defensive," producing a poetry "not projected outward into a world it would shape, but inward into a world it would protect" ("Authors-Readers: Jonson's Community of the Same," 56). But to establish or protect fragile goods (integrity, good sense, liberty, friendship, love of learning, self-knowledge, self-control, and the rest) in a world indifferent or hostile to them need not be a "negative" enterprise. Nor is it an easy or "superfluous" task to make such ideals vivid and active in the mind.

the recurring procession of the seasons. Cyclical and ahistoric, the Roman festival strives to recognize and participate in the eternal rhythms of the natural world and to enable its participants to maintain some perspective on the inevitable gap between nature and society, or to use Plato's words, *physis* and *nomos*. Under that dispensation the ultimate "vice" is ignorance, the ultimate "virtue" knowledge. But Jonson's "procession" is also progressive: from the present (and the past which created it) and into the future (which the present is now creating), the whole process to be superintended by memory, who is in this case the mother of truth. Here are not only the enlivening insights of a Martial, but also the vital connection missing for the childless Volpone, the exemplary action which encourages the capacity for further virtuous action in those who see and understand it. For Jonson, as for Sir Philip Sidney, the end of poetry is "well-doing" and not "well-knowing" only. As with Jonson's use of Ovid, the earlier poet's end has become part of the later's means.[22]

* * *

Having traced the major points of convergence and divergence from Martial, we must, before analyzing Jonson's book in detail, understand his idea of the form of the epigram, the "old way, and the true" which he claims to be restoring. His theory of the epigram is clear enough; his practice, in which he diverges from all previous epigrammatists (most notably in the final epigram, "The Famous Voyage") is more complicated. The beginning point for Jonson's understanding of the form seems to have been (as so often) his contemptuous rejection of contemporary epigrammatists, whom he believed to have perverted the epigram's proper purpose and technique. Prior to the outbreak of satire in the 1590s, the epigram had played a minor part in English poetry.[23] The English Neo-Latinists of the sixteenth century had written epigrams (Sir Thomas More's *Epigrammata* of 1518 being the first), some of which had appeared in a translation by Timothe Kendall

---

22. Claude Levi-Strauss's discussion of "bricolage" is relevant to Jonson's treatment of earlier writers (*The Savage Mind*, 16.16). See G. W. Pigman III, "Versions of Imitation in the Renaissance," 26, for the *aemulatio* that "calls attention to itself and deliberately challenges comparison with its model." On "imitation" in Jonson, see also Richard S. Peterson, *Imitation and Praise in the Poems of Ben Jonson,* ch. 1; and Thomas M. Greene, *The Light in Troy: Imitation and Discovery in Renaissance Poetry,* ch. 13.

23. On the contemporary context of the *Epigrammes*, see H&S, 2:342 ff.; T. K. Whipple, "Martial and the English Epigram from Sir Thomas Wyatt to Ben Jonson"; Hoyt H. Hudson, *The Epigram in the English Renaissance*; Rosalie Colie, *The Resources of Kind: Genre Theory in the Renaissance*; Alastair Fowler, *Kinds of Literature: An Introduction to the Theory of Genres and Modes*; Coiro, *Robert Herrick's Hesperides*, ch. 4.

Epic and Epigram 57

(1577). Although sometimes serious and moral,[24] these sought for the most part to imitate the descriptive and memorial graces of the *Greek Anthology* and were thus of little direct use to the satirists of the '90s. The same may be said of the proverbial and anecdotal "epigrams" produced by Heywood and Crowley in the middle of the century.

The collections of satiric epigrams that start appearing in the 1590s (Herford lists eight such collections from John Davies [1598] to John Harington [1613]) owe much to Martial, but, as Jonson thought and as most readers have agreed, their imitations are usually partial and tendentious. They often lack his urbanity and civilizing, judicial force, and often descend to personal or partisan abuse. Epigrams can be both personal and bitter, but the controlling purpose must tend to some more general good. How thoroughly poisonous and antisocial the reputation of epigrams had become may be seen in Jonson's reference to them in the dedication, where Pembroke is assured that he need not fear "though they [epigrams] carry danger in the sound." He addresses the same expectations more generally in "To My Booke":

> It will be look'd for, booke, when some but see
> Thy title, *Epigrammes,* and nam'd of mee,
> Thou should'st be bold, licentious, full of gall,
> Wormewood, and sulphure, sharpe, and tooth'd withall;
> Become a petulant thing, hurle inke, and wit,
> As mad-men stones: not caring whom they hit.
>
> (II.1-6)

Jonson, however, aspires to a "wiser temper" and to a tempered judgment—properly balancing all the relevant elements or "humours"—essential to the epigram, and so conspicuously missing in contemporary practice.

We know from the *Conversations with Drummond* that he reacted against deficiencies in the form as well as the manners of the epigram. Those who have explicitly considered its form all recognize two necessary components, variously described, that Lessing calls "Erwartung" and "Aufschluss": expectation and "unlocking" or conclusion.[25] For the epigram to

---

24. See Mary Thomas Crane, "*Intret Cato*: Authority and Epigram in Sixteenth Century England."

25. See Hudson, *The Epigram in the English Renaissance*, ch. 1, for a general discussion, and Smith, *Poetic Closure*, 196 ff. See also the first section of Lessing's "Ueber das Epigramm," in *Gesammelte Werke*, 7:7-51. Karen M. Holum observes that "the effect depends on the interruption of a series of parallel semantic units. . . . The reader is led to expect a completed set of parallels, until the pattern is destroyed by the discordant . . . unit

accomplish its end, both parts must be fully represented. Jonson objected specifically to two common violations of the form. Some lack a turn or point entirely and are, like those of John Owen, "bare Narrations," or like those of Sir John Harington, "Narrations, and not Epigrames" (*Conversations,* 223-25, 37-40). Others "expressed in the end what should have been understood by what was said" (*Conversations,* 381-82) and therefore lack sufficient point. Herford and Simpson justly observe, with regard to the first of these strictures, that the epigram must be capped by a reflection; but they do not sufficiently appreciate the force of the second when they characterize it as a demand "that the reflection shall not be quite obvious or otiose."[26] In fact, Jonson's conclusions are sometimes obvious. "On Lieutenant Shift" (XII), for example, spends 22 lines depicting the activities of a shiftless officer who acquits all his debts with the "charm" "God pays," concluding:

> But see! th'old baud hath serv'd him in his trim,
> Lent him a pockie whore. Shee hath paid him.
>
> (23-24)

Although Jonson's conclusions may be witty or surprising, what remains essential is that, even in such devices as this simple reversal, the turn should deliver a judgment, a definitive "naming" of the person or action in question. The point is not amusement but understanding, and this understanding should arise from a "ripening" effect implicit in epigram form. Exposition and conclusion present a kind of growth and harvest: the subject is explored, developed, fully "ripened" until ready to receive the cutting edge of judgment. The poems thus hold out the fruits of a mature (and maturing) consideration for our inspection and understanding. Each operates, in miniature, like the plays in which plot and character expand and develop to a point of complex interrelation that can only be "understood" in a court of judgment, whether literal (*Every Man in His Humour, Volpone*) or figurative (*Epicoene, The Alchemist, Bartholmew Fayre*).

Yet Jonson's phrase "the ripest of my studies" refers not primarily to individual epigrams, but to the collection as a whole. What sense can we make of this claim? A hundred odd epigrams are greater than *Volpone* or the historical tragedies on which Jonson lavished so much pride and effort? I think it is safe to say that no reader of Jonson will, or should, assent fully

---

which tells an unpalatable truth about life" ("The Epigram: Semantic Basis for the Pointed Ending," 36).

26. H&S, 2:351.

to this proposition. Yet there is a sense in which it is entirely accurate. To understand this claim, its force, and its limits, we must bear in mind the scope and resonances of the encompassing metaphors of battle and procession; the figure of the name-maker, that visionary demiurge and lawgiver, wrestling at the most fundamental level with the perceptions and responses that control the moral life; and the poet's determination to bring all the objects within the field of vision to a full and tempered judgment. Taken together these tend toward a poetic purpose and effect that is essentially heroic or epic, and only incidentally satiric, comic, elegiac, or encomiastic. As the epic was traditionally thought to contain other literary forms, so the underlying epic intentions of the *Epigrammes* contain many other local intentions and effects.

Let me make clear at once that I do not suggest that Jonson would have sought to compare this small collection with the epics of Homer, Virgil, Ariosto, Tasso, or Spenser. But like most of his contemporaries, Jonson had the epic itch, the desire to write the *magnum opus* that would do justice to the whole of his own experience and that of his nation and culture.[27] Such a work would be the ultimate achievement of the sort of public poet that Jonson always aspired to be. Virgil rather than Horace gains the highest honors in the poetic manifesto of the *Poetaster,* and one continually feels in the awkward prologues, epilogues, dialogues, and so on of the plays that Jonson is conscious of a depth of purpose straining against the boundaries of his forms. Here, perhaps for the first time, he finds a "theater" adequate to his richest purpose.

Renaissance ideas (and Jonson's ideas) of what might constitute epic or heroic poetry were less restricted than our own. Robert M. Durling has remarked that "with characteristic inventiveness the Renaissance developed many kinds of poetry it considered to be epic—historical, chivalric, Biblical, hagiographic, mythological, geographical, and so forth."[28] Herford observes that Jonson in the *Conversations with Drummond* is "full of epic

---

27. On Jonson's "laureate" ambitions, see Richard Helgerson, *Self-Crowned Laureates: Spenser, Jonson, Milton and the Literary System*. Helgerson prefers to see masque, rather than epigram, as "the supreme vehicle of Jonson's laureate self-realization" (172) and feels that Jonson's ambitions were frustrated because of "the inadequacy of the genres in which he worked" (173). While the masques were of course the more visible, the *Epigrammes* seem to me the more important (and finally successful) expression of Jonson's public role.

28. Robert M. Durling, *The Figure of the Poet in the Renaissance Epic*, 91. See also Brian Vickers, "Epideictic and Epic in the Renaissance," for the understanding of heroic poetry in rhetorical rather than formal terms.

schemes and notions" and demonstrates "a conception of Epic... very far from suggesting servile adherence either to Homer, Vergil, or Aristotle."²⁹ The prime exhibit is his *Heroologia*, described by Drummond as partly written by 1619 and later lost in the fire that destroyed Jonson's library in 1623. Drummond places it first of all the "Informations and maners" he records:

> that he had ane intention to perfect ane Epick Poeme intitled Heroologia of the Worthies of his Country, rowsed by fame, and was to dedicate it to his Country, it is all in Couplets, for he detesteth all other Rimes, said he had written a discourse of Poesie both against Campion & Daniel, especially this last, where he proves couplets to be the bravest sort of Verses, especially when they are broken, like Hexameters. (*Conversations*, 1–9)

This report establishes Jonson's thinking on the proper metrical structure for heroic poetry: "broken" couplets (those making full use of *caesura* and enjambment), which are used in all the *Epigrammes* save one.³⁰ Drummond's description is also interesting for the idea of epic structure implied by the whole project, as it was evidently intended as a plotless serial celebration of individual circumstances and accomplishments—i.e., a procession of heroes. It indicates that Jonson conceived the possibility of epic intention and effect being accomplished without benefit of the traditional epic action or "fable," employing instead a fragmentary method similar to that of the *Epigrammes*—though probably unified by chronology rather than by an omnipresent speaker—and omitting the nameless.³¹

Also available to him was the example of his "master," William Camden, whose *Britannia* was first published in 1586 and exerted a strong influence on Jonson's collection.³² The book is a serial examination of notable places, families, and other "names" throughout Britain, in which his purpose has been "to seeke, rake out, and free from darkenesse such places as *Caesar, Tacitus, Ptolomy, Antonine* the emperor, *Notitia Provin-*

---

29. H&S, 2:339.
30. The exception is the acrostic "On Margaret Ratcliffe" (XL).
31. Herford and Simpson point to the descriptions of Richard I, the Black Prince, and Henry V in *The Speeches at Prince Henry's Barriers* (1610) as likely indications of how Jonson might have proceeded (H&S, 1:152).
32. References in H&S, 11:620, show that Jonson used the book throughout his career. It should also be noted that Camden's *Remains Concerning Britain* (1605) contains antiquarian collections of, among other things, "impresses" of the nobility, epitaphs, and epigrams, of which Camden observes that "in short and sweet poems framed to praise or dispraise, or some sharp conceit, which are called Epigramms, as our countrymen now surpass other Nations, so in former times they were not inferiour" (344).

ciarum, & other antique writers have specified and *Time* hath overcast with mist & darknes by extinguishing, altering, & corrupting their old true names."³³ He defends his method, against those "which will apprehend it disdainfully & offensively that I have not remembered this or that family . . . but (only) such as hapned in my way according to the method I proposed to myself."³⁴ And then more generally:

> Others will call me in question for that I have commended some persons now living; yet I have done it sparingly, and that out of an assurance of verity, out of the common consent and voice of such as can well judge of worth, & from no base flattery. By these sparing commendations such as are commended may be lessoned that their deportments may be answerable, and that they preserve and daily increase the same. Succeeding ages, which I respect more than the present, will render to every man his right whatsoever is now scribbled in papers. In the mean time I wish them to remember that to praise good men is but to shew a light of direction as out of a watch towre to posteritie. True is that saying of *Symmachus, Imitation is encouraged with the seemely praises of the good, and imitating vertue is cherished by the example of others honour.*³⁵

Here then is a major work, of heroic scope, that points in purpose, method, and perspective to Jonson's efforts in the *Epigrammes* and *Heroologia.*

If Jonson and his contemporaries had a broader view of epic than we possess today, they had also a greater familiarity with and respect for the powers of epigram, since most were "trained in the writing of . . . the epigram, [which] with all its taxing problems of expression, was a major whetstone of poetic wit and wits."³⁶ The Italian critics and theorists were particularly interested in the form; some devoted entire treatises to it.³⁷ Francesco Robortello's *De Epigrammata* (1548), for example, treats the epigram as a plastic form, readily adapted to the special qualities of more fully determined genres, and gives examples of tragic, amatory and epic epigrams. Tommaso Correa, in his *De Toto eo poematis genere, quod epigramma vulgo dicitur Libellus* (1569), requires that the epigrammatist

---

33. William Camden, *Britain,* trans. Philemon Holland (London, 1637 [1610]), fol. 6r.
34. Ibid., fol. 5v. Compare Jonson's "To all, to whom I write" (IX):

> May none, whose scatter'd names honor my booke,
> For strict degrees of ranke, or title looke:
> 'Tis 'gainst the manners of an *Epigram*:
> And, I a *Poet* here, no *Herald* am.

35. Ibid., fol. 6r.
36. Rosalie Colie, *Shakespeare's Living Art,* 77.
37. Concerning the Italian critics, I rely on Bernard Weinberg, *A History of Literary Criticism in the Italian Renaissance*; for Robertello, see 1:400–401 and for Correa, 1:185–87.

possess in abundance the qualities of *imitatio* and *judicio,* and defines the epigram according to a rhetorical model involving the poet, those he addresses and tries to influence directly, and the larger audience affected by the whole collection. In these commentaries and in other works that discuss the epigram more briefly, it appears as a serious, flexible instrument that can be fitted to a variety of literary purposes—including the highest.[38]

What connection can there be between the expansiveness of the epic and the compression of the epigram? Minturno, with whose work Jonson was directly familiar (even adapting his description of the poet for a crucial passage in the dedication of *Volpone*), called the epigram a "tiny piece of epic poetry" (*particella dell'epica poesia*).[39] Indeed, there is a fundamental similarity in the determination of both epigrammatist and epic poet to engage their subjects as fully as possible, seeing them both as they are in themselves and as they signify in the larger pattern of life. The similarity is particularly well expressed in G. W. F. Hegel's *Aesthetics* (published posthumously in 1835), a product of that German neoclassicism that had already seen the appearance of Lessing's essay on the epigram. Hegel describes the first of two phases of the epigram (and of all art) as "objective": "in the oldest epigrams . . . we do not get the sketch of an object in association with some sentiment or other; we have the thing in itself in a double way: (a) the external existent and (b) then its meaning and explanation; these are pressed together as an epigram with the most salient and apposite touches."[40] The second phase is "subjective": "at this stage what is especially at stake is that the heart, with its depth of feeling, and the spirit and a rich consciousness shall be entirely absorbed in the circumstances, situation, etc., tarry there, and so make out of the object something new, beautiful and intrinsically valuable."[41] Dialectician that he is, Hegel particularly values art in which these qualities are held in fruitful tension—as

---

38. Fowler comments on "the broad extension of epigram, from the late sixteenth century to the early eighteenth" (*Kinds of Literature*, 195), an extension which "modulated" other forms, and "brought about changes in the very scale of literature. Textures were closer knit, so that what may be called literary events came to be expected in a work more frequently" (202).

39. Antonio Sebastiano Minturno, *L'Arte Poetica*, 281. Fowler cautions that the statement refers to the epigram's "presentational mode," not to its inclusion in the epic (*Kinds of Literature*, 218). In the dedication to *Volpone*, ll. 27-30, Jonson portrayed the poet as "the interpreter, and arbiter of nature, a teacher of things divine, no lesse than humane, a master in manners; and can alone (or with a few) effect the business of man-kind." Herford and Simpson (H&S, 9:683) give the passage from *De Poeta* (1558).

40. G. W. F. Hegel, *Aesthetics: Lectures on Fine Art*, 1:425.

41. Ibid., 610.

they are in the *Epigrammes,* where the mingled "objectivity" and "subjectivity" of the speaker, his "guarded vulnerability," gives the collection its special character. Hegel also suggests the connection between epigram and epic, and discusses the epic qualities that a collection of such fragments may attain. In his treatment of epic poetry, he begins with the "elementary epic," and after mentioning the epic character of epigraphs, *gnomoi, sententiae,* elegies, and so on, states that they

> may be lifted from their fragmentary character and independent separation, ranged together into a greater whole, and rounded off into a totality which is entirely of an epic sort. This is because in this totality the unity holding the parts together, and the real centre, is not provided by a purely lyrical mood or dramatic action but by a specific and real sphere of life, the essential nature of which is to be brought home to our minds both in its general character and also in its particular trends, aspects, occurrences, duties, etc. Conformably with this whole stage of epic, which exhibits the permanent and the universal as such with the chiefly ethical aim of warning, teaching, and summoning to an inherently sterling moral life, productions of this kind acquire a didactic tone . . . by allowing the descriptive element its necessary scope too, they prove completely that the whole of their doctrine and description is directly drawn from a reality that has been grasped in its substance and lived through.[42]

Hegel cites Hesiod's *Works and Days* as an example, but the description is of wider application.

Indeed, Hegel's analysis covers at once the most primitive and the most sophisticated forms of the epic, as our own century has come to see. M. L. Rosenthal and Sally M. Gall have described the "new" genre of "the modern sequence . . . a grouping of mainly lyric poems and passages, rarely uniform in pattern, which tend to interact as an organic whole. . . . Intimate, fragmented, self-analytical, open, emotionally volatile . . . even when the poet aspires to tragic or epic scope." In this genre, success depends upon an "ability to hold in balance conflicting and logically irreconcilable energies and to identify their presence and intensity," mastering contradictions to produce "a pattern of unruly but mobilized

---

42. Ibid., 2:1041-42. Paul Friedlaender points out that early Greek memorial inscriptions were intended as fragmentary imitations of the epic manner, because the people then "felt themselves and their dead akin to the heroes of Homer . . . verse transposed [their experience] into the representation of a Homeric or Hesiodic event and gave a 'heroic tinge' to everyday life" (*Epigrammata: Greek Inscriptions in Verse,* 7).

affects."[43] In the *Epigrammes,* Jonson aims at and largely achieves an "epic" of just this ancient and modern kind.

* * *

If Jonson's *Epigrammes* do then have epic pretensions, of what sort are they? In the dedication, Jonson identifies himself as one of the "studiers of *humanitie*" (38), and indeed, "humanitie" for worse and for better is his subject. Here as nowhere else in his works, he is concerned to do justice to both better and worse. The better, the "good and great names" to be led forth by Pembroke, we have already noticed, but the dedication gives equal attention to those who cry "*Beware the poet,* confessing, therein, so much love to their diseases, as they would rather make a partie for them, then be either rid or told of them" (12–15); those who will not "remit any thing of their riot, their pride, their self-love, and other inherent graces, to consider truth or vertue" (32–34). This triumvirate of "inherent graces" (i.e., original sins) represents the entire human personality in its diseased or fallen condition: "riot," the corruption of the body and senses; "pride," the corruption of the mind and spirit; "self-love," the corruption of the will and affections. As we have already seen, the last is for Jonson the most intimate, most powerful, and most pervasive of the three, and any consideration of "humanitie" must begin with its omnipresent effects. Thus we find a plentiful display of self-lovers in the greedy, fraudulent, lustful, self-regarding courtiers, courtesans, politicians, doctors, lawyers, soldiers, poets, critics, playwrights, usurers, and bawds who dominate the first half of the collection. Here the response to self-love is not the restraining, manipulative Crites of *Cynthias Revels,* nor the self-destructive machinations of the principals in *Volpone,* who "feed' until they "bleed," but instead the "lived through" response of actual men and women (and poets). Following Jonson's favorite antimasque/masque rhythm, the self-lovers who predominate in the first half are gradually and decisively (albeit incompletely) replaced in the second by those who live according to better principles and to better ends. Here as nowhere else, Jonson undertakes to demonstrate how, to borrow Bacon's metaphor again, one destroys the weeds and waters the herbs of nature in men.

Jonson begins to establish the terms of his analysis in the dedication and the first few introductory poems. The dedication is addressed

43. M. L. Rosenthal and Sally M. Gall, *The Modern Sequence: The Genius of Modern Poetry,* 9, 11. Neil Fraistat names Petrarch as the first modern poet to show "how a collection of diverse poems might itself aspire toward the complexity and variety of a long poem" (*Poems in Their Place: The Intertextuality and Order of Poetic Collections*, 6).

Epic and Epigram

TO THE GREAT
EXAMPLE OF
HONOR AND
VERTUE,
THE MOST NOBLE
WILLIAM
EARLE OF PEMBROKE,
L. CHAMBERLAYNE, &c.

MY LORD. While you cannot change your merit, I dare not change your title: It was that made it, and not I.

Much virtue in "&c." The very form of the address implies the critical distinction between true and false, significant and insignificant names: the "moral" names matter, the official titles can be mostly dispensed with. We are also introduced to the key ideas of change and contract. Pembroke's particular virtue here, as later in the epigram addressed to him, is that he does not "change," that his "noblesse keeps one stature still, / And one true posture, though besieg'd with ill" (CII.13–14). Jonson responds with a complementary keeping of faith: since you don't change your merit, I won't change your name—a pointed refusal in that this form of address is identical to that in the dedication to *Catiline,* the play immediately preceding in the *Workes.* The dedication and introductory poems (I-IV) are remarkable for the intensity with which both factors, change and contract, are made vivid.[44] We are plunged immediately into a whirl of changes, of shifting possibilities of tone, stance, action, and judgment. Pembroke is by turns subject, reader, and actor, both within and beyond the frame of the book; Jonson, in tones ranging from humility to sarcasm, light irony, dignified seriousness, and cheerful unseriousness, addresses the reader, the book (and the reader), the bookseller and his "judgment," and King James, who is within ten lines king, poet, reader, actor, and judge—thus one man in his poem plays many parts.[45] The effect of this exuberant variety and freedom of movement is to push the fact of change to the fore. If this work is to deal adequately in an "epic" way with "humanitie," it must address the primary reality governing all life: mutability. Change is many things, good and evil. As Richard S. Peterson has persuasively argued, however much

---

44. Partridge also notes the extraordinary energy and variety of the opening ("Jonson's *Epigrammes,*" 164).
45. On Jonson's relations with James I, see Leah S. Marcus, *The Politics of Mirth,* 9–13.

Jonson may have valued the stability of the "centered self," he is no advocate of stasis and immobility.[46] Rather, he eagerly embraces and practices exploration, assimilation, and growth, while rejecting and warning against the wasting, degrading metamorphosis of the narcissistic "famisht mind" that ransacks the whole world but never finds its proper food. The issue is not stasis versus change (for life is change), but how change is to be managed, directed, used.

Jonson's answer is not far to seek. For with an energy that matches the presentation of these shifting rhetorical possibilities, the speaker is also busy establishing contracts, reciprocal bonds of obligation, with Pembroke, with the reader, with himself and "his own honesty," with the bookseller, with King James. Thus, Jonson will tell unpopular truths, and Pembroke will protect him and gain greater honor; the reader will make an effort to understand, and the author undertakes that it is worth the trouble; the author does not want the book advertised, and the bookseller may dispose of the remainders as he sees fit; the poet will do homage to (and gracefully flatter) the king, and the king will test and approve the poet. Why is the idea of contract so important? Sir Edward Coke, the eminent jurist (and subject of a later epigram, *Under-wood*, XLVI), remarks that "in every contract there must be a *quid pro quo,* for *contractus est quasi actus contra actum.*"[47] "*Actus contra actum*": one action set against another; one action responding to another; one man responding, through his actions, to another—this is the basis for all moral and social life, for the lives of the virtuous in the *Epigrammes,* and for whatever hope Jonson holds for "humanitie." Jonson's "contract" is like Bacon's "custom," the ever adaptable response to "nature," but custom raised to a higher power. It governs (to the extent they can be governed) all the relations, all the changes in human life: patronage, poetry, business, politics, fatherhood, sonship, marriage, friendship, fellowship, past and present, present and future.

If the primary realities to be explored are, on the one hand, the nature and necessity of change, and on the other, the human and humanizing capacity for contract, the power of the mind that both perceives and governs these is judgment. The words "judge" and "judgment" appear several times

---

46. See Peterson, *Imitation and Praise*, 29–30, which corrects the overemphasis on stability in Greene's seminal "Ben Jonson and the Centered Self"; see also Greene's later "Accommodations of Mobility in the Poetry of Ben Jonson" in *The Light in Troy*.

47. Edward Coke, *The First Part of the Institutes of the Laws of England; Or, A Commentary upon Littleton*, fol. 47v.

in the book, and instances of judgment are everywhere.[48] Each epigram is a judgment upon what it describes, but beyond this, everyone is portrayed as continually engaged in acts of judgment—and Jonson himself first among them. In the dedication, he claims power as a poet to judge vicious and virtuous, and to express each justly. The reader, in turn, must understand well enough to judge properly. The public must not prejudge the contents of this book by its title. The bookseller who "Call's a booke good, or bad, as it doth sell" (III.2) has his own lesser, but nonetheless valid, basis for judging the "worth" of books. The poet will submit himself to "the best / Of Kings for grace; of *Poets* for my test?" (IV.9-10). Judgment is the divine spark in man; through the continual process of judging and submitting to judgment, he affirms what is best in his "humanitie" and keeps whole the contracts that bind him with others, with himself, and (however distantly) with God.[49]

Thus, Jonson establishes early the primary terms—change, contract, and a superintending judgment—before entering into the "action" of the *Epigrammes*. And it is well that he does, for in the first half of the collection (the first sixty epigrams or so), there will be few points of reference outside the speaker himself. Before we plunge into the maelstrom of self-love and self-deception, the swirl of unbridled change and metamorphosis, we find, placed like a gateway, Epigram V, "On the Union":

> When was there contract better driven by *Fate*?
> Or celebrated with more truth of state?
> The world the temple was, the priest a king,
> The spoused paire two realmes, the sea the ring.

Several things are accomplished here. The poem marks out the perimeter of the observations and action to follow: life within an established society. The traditional, presocial, epic tasks of founding and securing have been performed by the king and "celebrated" by him in a cosmic context; now the poet will celebrate and investigate the life within it. The ideal of "contract" is made explicit and characterized as the activity of Fate, the power that governs human destiny. Moreover, this is a "marriage," the most intimate and complete kind of contract, which transforms parts into a new whole

---

48. Preston, "Verse Concordance," 1622. "Judge" appears ten times, as verb or noun; "judgment" and "just," seven apiece.

49. See Jennifer Brady, "Jonson's 'To King James': Plain Speaking in the *Epigrammes* and the *Conversations*," 389: "[in] the educative process of Jonson's *Epigrammes* . . . moral self-scrutiny stands as the secular equivalent to divine judgment."

and give rise to new life. Thus we begin with an image of wholeness in the body politic, a rite celebrated by its "head," King James, a wholeness which will contrast with the ensuing fragmentation of the body political and physical, Jonson's recurring metaphor for the disintegrating, metamorphic effects of change. Interesting too is his inversion of usual epigrammatic procedure by beginning with the judgment or comment and concluding with the image of the paired realms "ringed" by the sea—perhaps implicitly recognizing (as he will also at the end of the book) that in poetry it is the image or vision that must finally validate the judgment.

Once past this opening image of completeness, things begin to happen quickly. We meet in the next eight poems alchemists, whores, a thief, a shifty soldier, an incompetent doctor, and corrupt, ignorant and ineffectual courtiers. Some are seen and judged in the brevity of two lines, while one is stretched to twenty-four. Some are "on" their subjects, others directly addressed "to" their subjects.[50] Yet beyond the rapid and unpredictable shifts in subject, length, and rhetorical distance, what is most striking here and throughout the first part dominated by the satirized self-lovers is a certain teasing quality, of things irritatingly half-formed and half-related; of mocking juxtapositions, inversions, direct and ironic half-parallels and half-references; of a subworld of actions and agents inextricably bound to each other, yet incoherent.[51] Thus, the "great art" pretended by alchemists, the illusory alchemical "marriage" of the elements, follows the true marriage arranged by King James. The "Hot-house" that follows glances ironically at both "marriage" and the glass retorts (one might say, forcing beds) of the alchemists. "Hot-house" and "whore-house" are found to be "Synonima" in VII, as "courtier" and "thief" become synonyms in VIII. Mention of the court brings a distinction between "Herald" and "Poet" in IX, which in turn leads to the Ignorant Lord of X and the "Some-thing that walkes Some-where" of XI. The Lieutenant Shift who contracts the pox in XII is followed by the quack "Doctor Empirick" in XIII, who gives way to the truly learned man, William Camden, in XIV. This list could be continued indefinitely and even varied considerably with regard to the points of connection; for these poems abound in small and large similarities and differences, and the intensity and significance of the juxtapositions varies

50. Partridge, "Jonson's *Epigrammes*," discusses the varied intimacy and distance achieved by frequent alternations of "on" and "to."

51. Edmund Wilson similarly observes (unfavorably) of the plays that Jonson's "juxtapositions of elements are . . . often like the 'mechanical mixtures' of chemistry that produce no molecular reactions" ("Morose Ben Jonson," in *The Triple Thinkers*, 216).

Epic and Epigram 69

unpredictably. The poems are juxtaposed in such a way that they seem, like the people they describe, opportunist and parasitical. They mirror, in their imperfect relatedness, their subjects' imperfect awareness of themselves and of the implications of their actions.

These satiric epigrams richly display the "riot, pride, and self-love" promised in the dedication. Yet Jonson is engaged in more than name-making and name-calling, for he supports his moral analysis with an effective pattern of metaphor involving metamorphosis, the change or loss of "shape." Again the epigram addressed to Pembroke shows the forces at work:[52]

>   in this strife
> Of vice, and vertue; wherein all great life
> Almost, is exercis'd: and scarse one knowes,
> To which, yet, of the sides himselfe he owes.
> They follow vertue, for reward, to day;
> To morrow vice, if shee give better pay:
> And are so good, and bad, just at a price,
> As nothing else discernes the vertue' or vice.
>   (CII.5-12)

The emphasis is on moral instability and confusions of identity. Indeed, metamorphosis, prominently associated with the similar mutability of the passions and the human body, is generally treated as the concomitant of vice. There is no place here for the enlivening and awakening metamorphoses of Shakespeare and others.[53] As in *Volpone*, metamorphosis is an image of the change and decay that besets human life, passion, and purpose, and represents the main threat to moral and social order. Sir Voluptuous Beast, for example, typical in his oxymoronic name (Sir-Beast) of the rational animal, man, proceeds through a degrading series of changes in corrupting his wife:

> While Beast instructs his faire, and innocent wife,
> In the past pleasures of his sensuall life,

---

52. Forces also at work within Pembroke himself, whom the *DNB* describes, following Clarendon, as, on the one hand, "most universally loved and esteemed of any man of his age . . . always ready to advance worthy men . . . [one who] maintained an honourable independence amid court factions . . . [and was] a great lover of his country"; but on the other, as a man "unhappy in domestic affairs," who "lacked force of character" as a statesman, and whose mind was weakened by "immoral indulgences."

53. For other contemporary treatments of the theme, see, for example, Reuben A. Brower, *The Fields of Light*, ch. 6; and Cyrus Hoy, "Shakespeare, Sidney, and Marlowe: The Metamorphosis of Love."

> Telling the motions of each petticote,
> And how his GANIMEDE mov'd, and how his goate,
> And now, her (hourely) her owne cucqueane makes,
> In varied shapes, which for his lust shee takes:
> What doth he else, but say, leave to be chast,
> Just wife, and, to change me, make womans hast?
>   (XXV)

Notice here the "just wife" corrupted from her proper "shape" and proper obligations by the degrading force of self-regarding desire. As with Celia and Volpone, the contending forces are justness and the metamorphic pleasures of the diseased, narcissistic imagination. Like that of Narcissus and Volpone, Beast's self-love, unrestrained, is finally self-destructive: in teaching his wife to change from what she should be, he will himself be changed to what he would not be—a cuckold. The danger to the human personality comes not only from passionate metamorphosis of the "Guts" and "Groynes," but also from the passionless amorphousness of such as the "Some-thing, that walkes Some-where" (XI), a courtier who is all looks, clothes, faces, and seeming, but will neither do good nor dare ill. Refusing the essential "strife," he is left to "walke dead still."

The challenge of metamorphosis will not be fully met until the second half, where we will see those, Pembroke prominent among them, who know how to keep their "shape" or "posture." But within this shifting, teasing, degrading variety, some continuity is provided by the regularity of the verse (all couplets), the regularity of the epigram structure, and by the speaker's recurring satisfaction as he transfixes each specimen with a pin through the center and places it in the collection. At the same time, a quiet, persistent counter-rhythm of integration is building as the speaker continually defines (and refines) himself as poet and as man.[54] He is, in the first place, no "*Herald*" concerned with "strict degrees of ranke, or title," but a "*Poet*" (IX)—that is, his judgments are not socially determined; and he has both the independence and angry inclination to pay back or "revenge" himself on the Ignorant Lord of X who does not appreciate the dignity of poetry. Since he wishes for his poems "a legitimate fame," he gladly submits

---

54. Durling notes that, in the epic, "a narrator's self-projection reflects an entire conception of man" (*Figure of the Poet*, 8). Cf. Louis L. Martz's comment on the narrator's self-projection in *Paradise Lost*, which "represents a motion forward to the time when the figure of the poet, representing the individual consciousness of man, will become the only organizing center for the long poem" (*Milton: Poet of Exile*, 79). I suggest that for Jonson that time had already arrived.

them to the judgment of the "learned Critick" of XVII. But he immediately turns in ferocious scorn upon the "Meere English Censurer" (i.e., one ignorant of Martial) who has "seene / DAVIS, and WEEVER, and the best have beene" (XVIII.3-4) and who is left to "beleeve still, and not judge so fast" because his "knowledge" is merely "faith" in others' opinions. The issue in these and similar poems is again judgment: who is qualified to judge and what is the basis for judgment? The speaker, *qua* poet, energetically judges others, yet is prepared to be judged by those who have a claim to equal or superior knowledge: the king, Camden, John Donne, and the learned generally. Thus, he thematically reinforces the formal properties of the epigram and makes the collection an arena or court of judgment in which none, particularly not the poet himself, is immune to judgment. This is the first check upon self-love.

The second check, scattered throughout the first half, arises in the poems of sonship, fatherhood, and friendship that establish Jonson's connections as a man. Here is no Volpone, "childless, rich," but rather one embedded in a rich network of personal contracts and payments.[55] In the second half, social responsibilities will come to the fore, and we will find the praises of statesmen, patrons and others. Here the praise is more intimate, more thorough, and involves the poet more deeply. It is that much more effective for being juxtaposed with the worst examples of irresponsible self-love. In these poems, Jonson portrays himself primarily as a keeper of contracts, a payer of debts. In the first poem, the noble tribute to his teacher Camden, he begins by acknowledging the one "to whom I owe / All that I am in Arts, all that I know" (XIV.1-2). In XXVII, he is obliged to provide "ornaments" for the hearse of his friend, Sir John Roe. He repays Beaumont for his praises (LV) and confesses himself inadequate to giving Donne his due praise: "all which I meant to praise, and, yet, I would; / But leave, because I cannot as I should" (XXIII.9-10). Particularly moving versions of this omnipresent theme occur in the epitaphs on his children, where he consoles himself (or tries to console himself) with the thought that their death is only one more debt he must pay. As he expresses it in "On My First Daughter" (XXII), "Yet, all heavens gifts, being heavens due, / It makes the father, lesse, to rue" (3-4). In the more anguished and complex "On My First Sonne" (XLV), he initially reflects that "Seven yeeres tho'wert lent to me, and I thee pay, / Exacted by thy fate, on the just day." Throughout, the

---

55. Gardiner, *Craftsmanship in Context*, ch. 2, also notes the prominence of ideas of "payment" and "reciprocity."

metaphor of contract and payment is analogous in structure to that of ripeness and judgment. Education, friendship, fatherhood, even life itself, are all taken "on contract"—a contract which in due time requires payment in gratitude, loyalty, praise, blame, death, grief, understanding.

Yet there is nothing cold or mechanical in these "transactions." The conclusion of the epigram to Camden sounds the characteristic note:

> Pardon free truth, and let thy modestie,
> Which conquers all, be once over-come by thee.
> Many of thine this better could, then I,
> But for their powers, accept my pietie.
>
> (XIV.11–14)

Here is mutual regard, mutual modesty, mutual respect for the truth—and the Virgilian final word is exactly right, for the Jonsonian speaker is sustained by the same kinds of relations and contracts which sustained "pius Aeneas" in his wanderings.[56] For Jonson, as for Virgil, the central problem is maintaining "shape": self-awareness and self-control directed to a humane purpose outside the self and maintained in the face of the ever-present, ever-prompting self-love and self-deception. His chief resource is similarly the sense of connection: the devoted son preserving what is deepest and best of the past, the father laboring for his children, aiding and aided by his friends and companions. Similar too is the promised reward: a new, universal city, based in law and justice, awareness and understanding.

The second half of the collection begins to trace such a renewed "city," a society of the virtuous contrasting with the promiscuous non-society of the first. But before it can be built in earnest, "Jonson" both as poet and man must pass a crisis as sharp, if not so extended, as Aeneas' journey to the underworld. He too must return to the source of poetic authority, must *antiquam exquirite matrem*—in this case, his Muse. "To My Muse" (LXV) occurs very near the midpoint of the book, where the dominant mood shifts from satire to encomium; where the virtuous outnumber (though never quite extinguish) the vicious in the same proportion as they were outnumbered in the first half;[57] where those praised have primarily social, political, or professional rather than personal connections with Jonson. The immedi-

---

56. W. H. Herendeen observes that "Camden . . . is the only true exemplar in the *Epigrammes*; as the type of virtue and wisdom he is the font of all the arts that adorn humanity, and in his relation to Jonson he sets the pattern for social order based on duty, reverential respect, intellectual honesty, and moral judgment" ("Like a Circle Bounded," 154).

57. See Partridge, "Jonson's *Epigrammes*," 171.

Epic and Epigram   73

ate context of this transitional self-examination is provided by three epigrams in praise of that consummate politician, Robert Cecil, the Earl of Salisbury.[58] They must be among the prickliest poems of praise on record. In the first (XLIII), we find the poet painfully self-conscious:

> What need hast thou of me? or of my *Muse*?
> Whose actions so themselves doe celebrate;
> Which should thy countries love to speake refuse,
> Her foes enough would fame thee, in their hate.
> 'Tofore, great men were glad of *Poets:* Now,
> I, not the worst, am covetous of thee.
> Yet dare not, to my thought, lest hope allow
> Of adding to thy fame; thine may to me,
> When, in my booke, men reade but CECILL's name,
> And what I write thereof find farre, and free
> From servile flatterie (common *Poets* shame)
> As thou stand'st cleere of the necessitie.

Is this praise at all? The lines are so roughly broken, so full of suppressed violence ("refuse, foes, hate, covetous, servile, shame"), the praise so negatively and grudgingly expressed, the poet so much more interested in his own motives than in Cecil's virtues, that one feels that the thrust of the epigram lies almost entirely in the first line: "What need hast thou of me? or of my *Muse*?" What is the relation of power to poetry? A man like Cecil raises special problems for Jonson's whole project. It is easy enough to praise Camden, or Lucy, Countess of Bedford, who is "Of greatest bloud, and yet more good then great" (LXXVI.6); easy enough to blame Don Surly, Fine Grand, and Sir Voluptuous Beast. But what to do with a politician like Cecil, a powerful man who does both good and ill, good for the state and ill to individual men and women? According to Drummond, Jonson said that "Salisbury never cared for any man longer nor he could make use of him" and that Jonson had once felt himself slighted at Salisbury's table (*Conversations*, 353–54, 317–21). Bacon wrote that in Salisbury's time, "able men were by design and of purpose suppressed."[59] Like the satirist who punishes the vice but leaves the man, the encomiast must sometimes find a way to praise the work but leave the man. Thus the second epigram to Cecil (LXIII), after briefly considering his active "virtue" (for which we might

---

58. I have discussed Jonson's epigrams to Cecil at greater length in "'What need hast thou of me? or of my *Muse*?': Jonson and Cecil, Politician and Poet."

59. In a letter of 1616, quoted in H&S, 1:167. As a frequent antagonist of the Cecils, both father and son, Bacon is, of course, hardly a disinterested judge.

well read Machiavelli's *virtù*), his lonely strength of character, and the King's "judgment" in using him, concludes:

> [Who] can to these be silent, *Salisburie*,
> Without his, thine, and all times injurie?
> Curst be his *Muse,* that could lye dumbe, or hid
> To so true worth, though thou thy selfe forbid.
>
> (9–12)

Attention is again deflected from Salisbury to the poet and his responsibilities, which must be fulfilled even, if necessary, against the secretive Salisbury himself.[60] The next epigram, the third (LXIV), which immediately precedes "To My Muse," is even subtler in its strategy. The first eight lines detail the reasons for which he is *not* writing; the next six pointedly praise the happy time of King James, "Where merit is not sepulcher'd alive" (10). Cecil himself appears almost as a graceful afterthought:

> These (noblest CECIL) labour'd in my thought,
> Wherein what wonder see thy name hath wrought?
> That whil'st I meant but thine to gratulate,
> I'have sung the greater fortunes of our state.
>
> (15–18)

This seems exactly right. The compliment to Cecil's power, particularly the power of his name—in his case, this is no mere poetic conceit—is precise, and to subsume the power and effect, the "art" of the politician (morally dubious as he often is) to the "greater fortunes of our state" is perhaps the best accommodation of this anomaly that can be expected. Jonson seems to have successfully negotiated Scylla and Charybdis, praising Cecil for what he contributed to the public good, without committing himself to Cecil as a man. He has not flattered him, nor has he avoided the imputation of flattery by the easy (and dangerous) device of some subterranean irony at Cecil's expense.[61] So much the more surprising, then, is the radical self-questioning of "To My Muse" (LXV):

> Away, and leave me, thou thing most abhord,
> That hast betray'd me to a worthlesse lord;

---

60. B. N. De Luna (*Jonson's Romish Plot: A Study of* Catiline *and its Historical Context,* 67–68) reads the poem as a declaration of Jonson's intent to celebrate Cecil's role in the Powder Plot. This seems unnecessarily specific, though the general analogy between Cecil and Cicero in *Catiline* is clear.

61. He did, after all, send autographs of these poems to Cecil; copies of XLIII and LXIII are among the Cecil Papers at Hatfield (H&S, 8:7).

> Made me commit most fierce idolatrie
> To a great image through thy luxurie.
> Be thy next masters more unluckie *Muse*,
> And, as thou'hast mine, his houres, and youth abuse.
> Get him the times long grudge, the courts ill will;
> And, reconcil'd, keepe him suspected still.
> Make him loose all his friends; and, which is worse,
> Almost all wayes, to any better course.
> With me thou leav'st an happier *Muse* then thee,
> And which thou brought'st me, welcome povertie.
> Shee shall instruct my after-thoughts to write
> Things manly, and not smelling parasite.
> But I repent me: Stay. Who e're is rais'd,
> For worth he has not, He is tax'd, not prais'd.

In context, the association of the terms "worthlesse lord" and "great image" with Cecil seems inescapable.[62] Yet how can it be so when we have seen Jonson so jealously and skillfully struggling to maintain his integrity while fulfilling his social purpose in a radically imperfect world?

Here it seems that a lesser victory has led to a larger challenge: having survived the crisis of the moral categories, the inadequacy of "good and great," "vice and virtue" to encompass fully the phenomenon of a Cecil, he now faces the crisis of poetry itself. What claim of special authority does the poet have? If he cannot trust his muse or himself to see and judge properly, what point is there to this book, and what hope for either poet or reader to master the whirl of competing interests and impressions that experience presents? Although he may provisionally adopt the mask of the satirist, the encomiast, the *magister* and *arbiter,* he is, after all, no poetic or Platonic demiurge, but a man, who must live within, not merely observe and comment upon, human life. How can he be sure he is not at times only a more refined "Parasite, or sub-parasite?" It is a crucial question for Jonson, who was, among other things, the most successful gatherer of patronage of

---

62. Richard Dutton suggests that Epigrams LVIII-LXV form a "sequence" in which "by implication and inference" Jonson makes "accusations . . . of guilt and unworthiness" against Salisbury and Mounteagle (*Ben Jonson: To the First Folio*, 145). This seems quite arbitrary: why not extend the "sequence" to impugn the praises of Carý (LXVI) or Suffolk (LXVII), or use "On Poet-Ape" (LVI) to undermine the praise of Beaumont (LV)? Jonson's method of association, juxtaposition, and contrast is directed not to the suggestion of (lightly) concealed ironies and indictments, but to the education of the reader in making often difficult discriminations and judgments. The effective statesmen shine all the brighter for their proximity to the spies, the "base stuff" of LIX.

his day[63]—and he has been conscious of it from the beginning. In the dedication, he remarks defensively that "if I have praysed, unfortunately, any one, that doth not deserve; or, if all answere not, in all numbers, the pictures I have made of them: I hope it will be forgiven me, that they are no ill pieces, though they be not like the persons" (21-25). A similar idea appears in "To My Booke":

> He that departs with his owne honesty
> For vulgar praise, doth it too dearely buy.
> (II.13-14)

But how can the poet aspire to his heroic purpose? How can he be trusted when he cannot trust himself? Is this book to be finally no more than a tissue of flattery and sarcastic self-importance? All those praised are in some degree imperfect; Cecil is only the most conspicuous and intransigent example of the impossibility of adequate "naming."

When faced with a difficulty, Jonson, like any good logician, makes a distinction. He will have a second muse. If the first was high, "luxurious," easily deceived by appearances, she will be corrected by a second who will be low, poor, and given to "after-thoughts" like the one which ends the poem. The technique of the epigram is thus turned upon the epigrammatist himself and in the most thorough and intimate way: he confesses the difficulty and submits to judgment. This awareness of his own imperfection separates the moralist from the moralizer and entitles him to praise a perfection that he can only imperfectly fit to his own experience of actual men and women.[64] Unlike the Platonic name-maker, who bears responsibility for any discontinuity between name and thing, the poet as moralist may demand that the subject live up to the name. The good he can pronounce absolutely; *who* is good only provisionally. Life must correct and complete the inevitable "imperfections" of art—or stand exposed by that art.[65] Having passed this validating crisis and having achieved an essential clarification of his own role and purpose, the poet's heroic effort to build through "naming," through myriad exemplary occasions of obser-

---

63. On Jonson's patronage, see Phoebe Sheavyn, *The Literary Profession in the Elizabethan Age*. David Norbrook observes that James I gave "enormous influence to one poet, Ben Jonson" (*Poetry and Politics in the English Renaissance*, 196).

64. Harris Friedberg observes that Jonson frequently presents "two poets, the speaker or putative poet unequal to his task and the actual poet . . . who succeeds by acknowledging poetic weakness" ("Ben Jonson's Poetry: Pastoral, Georgic, Epigram," 115).

65. Bruce R. Smith observes that "The epigram portrait 'of' a good man is directed 'to' good men, 'against' bad men: it becomes a standard that defines the onlookers as it defines the subject" ("Ben Jonson's *Epigrammes*," 104). See also Leggatt, *Ben Jonson*, 263; and William E. Cain, "The Place of the Poet in Jonson's 'To Penshurst' and 'To My Muse.'"

vation and judgment, a society of the "good and great" can begin in earnest. His authority has been restored (and even increased) by acknowledging its necessary limits. The poet who seeks authoritatively to "name the good" will fall short (his objects and instrument being both radically imperfect), as will the hero who seeks to build an eternal city. This crisis passed, the speaker begins modestly to build a better commonwealth—one in which goodness, warily allied with greatness, can predominate even if it cannot triumph—brick by brick, poem by poem. This process is no simpleminded substitution of praise for blame, virtuous for vicious. Gut and Groyne will still be jostling with the gentry at the end, and even the thoroughly admired and memorably praised Lucy, Countess of Bedford, will be warned against "that solemn vice of greatnesse, pride." But now the elements begin to support and reinforce each other, their individual patterns becoming additive rather than destructive or indifferent. What is essential is that smaller and larger patterns cohere, and Jonson takes care in most cases to make the praise both as perfectly individual and as perfectly general as possible. Consider for example Epigram LXX, "To William Roe":

> When *Nature* bids us leave to live, 'tis late
> Then to begin, my ROE: He makes a state
> In life, that can employ it; and takes hold
> On the true causes, ere they grow too old.
> Delay is bad, doubt worse, depending worst;
> Each best day of our life escapes us, first.
> Then, since we (more then many) these truths know:
> Though life be short, let us not make it so.

It is a classic admonition on the interrelation of life, labor, and independence, containing within eight lines no fewer than five sententiae (1–2, 2–4, 5, 6, and 8) and moving from confident summary to pointed admonition. Yet it also establishes bonds of affection and common situation between the older, who speaks, and the younger, who listens. Beyond its generic perfection lies the actual relation between Jonson and Roe, a younger friend for whom Jonson had recently (1610) had to testify in a lawsuit to recover some property imprudently sold. Jonson plays the older brother to perfection but without patronizing Roe. In addition, the poem is richer still for the "learned" critic who knows that the main ideas have been adapted from other classic "advices" by Seneca and Virgil.[66] The present advice is thus

---

66. Herford and Simpson (H&S, 11:12–13) compare with the first two lines of Epigram LXX Seneca's "Quam serum est tunc vivere incipere cum desinendum est!" (*De Brevitate Vitae*, 3.5); and with the fifth, "Maxima porro vitae iactura dilatio est. . . . Maximum vivendi impedimentum est expectatio, quae pendet ex crastino, perdit hodiernum" (Ibid.,

shaped from pieces of past advice; what sounds like the "superior" wisdom of the speaker is actually the shared wisdom of all such speakers and all such hearers. The reader who reads well understands not only the poem, good as it is, but also the connections, the contracts between older and younger, Jonson and Roe, ancient and modern, author and reader, that have formed it and which it forms in its turn.

While William Roe is advised to "make a state" in life, more often Jonson praises others for "keeping" a "state," or "shape," or "standing."[67] Contrary to the vicious metamorphosis of some and the sterile amorphousness of others, these people maintain their shapes, fulfilling their personal and social obligations, as does Pembroke, the exemplar:

> But thou, whose noblesse keeps one stature still,
> And one true posture, though besieg'd with ill
> Of what ambition, faction, pride can raise;
> (CII.13–15)

"On Sir John Roe" (XXXII) similarly contrasts the "often change of clime" undergone by the soldier with the steadfastness of his mind. Sir John Radcliffe (XCIII) "stand'st" "like a columne," "the great marke of vertue." Sir Thomas Roe (XCVIII) is told, "Thou hast begun well, ROE, which stand well too, / And I know nothing more thou hast to doo." Sir Edward Herbert (CVI) is praised for "standing upright to [him]selfe"; Sir Henry Nevil (CIX) for striving "To make thy lent life, good against the *Fates*: / And first to know thine owne state, then the States"; Sir William Jephson (CXVI) as the one who "stood'st up the master-braine" and "mad'st merit know her strength." William Roe is advised (CXXVIII) to be

> that good AENEAS, past through fire,
> through seas, stormes, tempests: and imbarqu'd for hell,
> Came back untouch'd. This man hath travail'd well.
> (12–14)[68]

9.1). Regarding Jonson's sixth line, they cite Virgil's "Optima quaeque dies miseris mortalibus aevi/prima fugit" (*Georgics*, 3.66–67), and mention Seneca's discussion of the passage (*Epistles*, 108.24–28). Ian Donaldson suggests further parallels in Horace and Martial (*Ben Jonson: Poems*, 38).

67. Greene observes that "virtually all the heroes and heroines . . . of the verse seem to possess [a] quality of fixed stability" ("Ben Jonson and the Centered Self," 330).

68. See the fine analysis of the poem in Peterson, *Imitation and Praise*, 33–43.

Epic and Epigram

To stand, to make, to know, and to keep one's state is the virtue of the man in the body politic. The capacity for making and keeping contracts and obligations with others and with oneself forms the civilizing bulwark against the destructive metamorphoses of the physical body, otherwise ruled by a self-love that refuses to pay what it does, in fact, "owe": thus the Lieutenant Shift (XII) who pays no one; the Fine Grand (LXXIII) who will not pay the poet; the Gut (CXVIII) who "in his belly, can . . . change a sin, / Lust it comes out, that gluttony went in." Only those who stand or pay perceive the real conditions upon which the life of the body of man, physical and political, rests. In the true economy that governs human life, and is imitated in the *Epigrammes,* there is place for neither tragedy (you pay for more than you get) nor romance (you get more than you pay for), but only for a strict comic justice. The proper part of man in this condition is—as many are said to do, and as the speaker is *shown* doing—to keep himself upright, neither grudging nor evading the inevitable settlement of accounts, but participating fully in the process of judgment, confident not only that it is the way of the world, but also, properly employed, the way to whatever health and civility are possible. It is man's chance to make the happiness he does not find.

Coincident with the ever clearer enunciation of moral and social principles are the progressively finer, larger definitions of the significance and purposes of poetry. Consider, for example, the majestic epigram (one almost thinks of it as an ode), "To Sir Henrie Savile" (XCV). Savile, who had translated and supplemented Tacitus' *Histories* (1591), is the most prominent of the three historians praised in the *Epigrammes.*[69] The poem begins, curiously enough, with the same notion that had animated Mosca's diverting "invention" in *Volpone,* Act I, scene ii:

> If, my religion safe, I durst embrace
> That stranger doctrine of PYTHAGORAS,
> I should beleeve, the soule of TACITUS
> In thee, most weighty SAVILE, liv'd to us.
>   (1-4)

Jonson has, as he says, little interest in the speculative doctrine of the transmigration of souls, but he is vitally interested in the actual transmigration of souls that takes place all the time in the tradition of the humanities, or "studie of humanitie." In this continuing spiritual "transmigration,"

---

69. The others are Camden (XIV) and Clement Edmonds (CX and CXI), translator of Caesar's commentaries (1600).

Savile has performed double service, "translating" his "original" fully, "both of sense, and sounds," and supplying a fateful gap in the historical record. He embodies Jonson's own attitude toward the ancients, loving them greatly and loving the truth more. Typically, he wishes that Savile would turn his attention—as had Camden, Drayton, and Jonson himself—to "matter of England,"[70] for Savile is peculiarly well situated to see and judge the times:

> For who can master those great parts like thee,
> That liv'st from hope, from feare, from faction free;
> That hast thy brest so cleere of present crimes,
> Thou need'st not shrinke at voyce of after-times.
>   (17–20)

His clarity of vision and purity of judgment rival the poet's own. This is not to say that the historian is superior to the poet or even that they are entirely at one; certainly Jonson would not have abated one jot of the superior freedom and dignity of poetry claimed by Sidney. But even as historians have come to see that interpretations of history are perhaps closer to poetry than was once imagined, so Jonson recognizes that a poetry attempting to interpret and guide human experience must be based in a historical sensibility, an attention to life as it is lived and has been lived. This provokes the final reflection on the nature of humane letters:

> Although to write be lesser then to doo,
> It is the next deed, and a great one too.
> We need a man that knowes the severall graces
> Of historie, and how to apt their places;
> Where brevitie, where splendor, and where height,
> Where sweetnesse is requir'd, and where weight;
> We need a man, can speake of the intents,
> The councells, actions, orders, and events
> Of state, and censure them: we need his pen
> Can write the things, the causes, and the men.
> But most we need his faith (and all have you)
> That dare nor write things false, nor hide things true.
>   (25–36)

Clearly, the historian has much in common with the epigrammatist. Both need unusual powers of exposition ("speake," "write") and judgment ("cen-

---

70. For Jonson's nearly completed "storie" of Henry V, see "An Execration Upon VULCAN" (*Under-wood* XLIII.97–100).

sure"); both must be masters of variety, present to all occasions; both must penetrate and link the surface and the depth, correctly tracing their "orders" of cause, effect, and countereffect; both must be masters of "things, causes, and men," able like wise magistrates to "censure" all they find. Yet this is not the end, for in the final couplet Jonson returns subtly and strikingly to the concerns of the opening lines. The final issue is "faith"—again not in a religious or metaphysical sense, but faith in the power and value of truth, understood as the bond, the "troth" that men establish with each other by speaking honestly what they know. The finding, expressing, and maintaining of this "truth" is the way in which the poet keeps his "faith," his "piety." The requirements of "writing" and "doing" are at bottom the same.[71]

We may also remember here Camden's similar project in his *Britannia* to search out the old "true names" of English places. In one sense, the enterprise is absurd. To imagine that towns or hills or stretches of seacoast have "true names" seems yet another version of the vague notion of Plato's *Cratylus* that there is some mystic "true" connection between names and things. But the "skill and faith in things," for which Jonson praises Camden and which raises his antiquarianism to the level of a moral force, is not so much a naive faith in the primitive coherence of names and things (though that may enter at times) as a desire to keep pure the collective memory and terminology, to insure that succeeding generations should call things by the same names and thus be able to understand and respond to each others' experience. This is the ongoing contract of the humane tradition, the symposium of past, present, and future affirming a common humanity in the teeth of riot, pride, self-love, and change.[72]

As earlier in the collection we saw the consolations of friendship, here we see its pleasures in shared understanding, shared enjoyment. Compare, for example, the first poem to John Donne (XXIII) with the second (XCVI). In the first, Jonson praises conventionally and worries (quite rightly) about the adequacy of the praise; in the second, he confidently sends his poems to Donne for judgment, while playfully imitating Donne's own verse mannerisms. He concludes with a line that pointedly expresses the likeness and

---

71. As in "To William Roe," there is a bonus for the learned reader. The last six lines of the poem paraphrase Cicero's own description of the ideal historian, and thus Savile, the historian of Rome, is praised as the man the Romans themselves had wished for. The idea of "faith" is Jonson's addition. See H&S, 11:19.

72. Joseph H. Summers observes that Jonson "seems to have found in his combination of roughly neo-stoic ethic and neo-classic aesthetic a major sustaining force analogous to what Donne discovered within the Church" (*The Heirs of Donne and Jonson*, 35).

unlikeness of the two friends: "A man should seeke great glorie, and not broad." How thoroughly Donne would have agreed and as thoroughly differed by pursuing a transcendent "glorie."[73]

This simultaneous celebration of similarities and differences in true friendship appears also in the poems to Jonson's patroness and friend, Lucy, Countess of Bedford. He remarks in sending her Donne's Satires (XCIV) that "Rare poemes aske rare friends." That the converse is also true we may see in LXXVI, "On Lucy Countesse of Bedford," in which the poet's project of "making" an ideal creature and a poem worthy of her are both solved in the last line by the epiphany of her name: "My *Muse* bad, *Bedford* write, and that was shee." In its elegant fusion of formality and familiarity, the poem testifies to a rare relation indeed between poet and patron. Like that to Pembroke, it is also an "epigram on all mankind"; as that describes what man must do, this describes what man might be:

> This morning, timely rapt with holy fire,
>   I thought to forme unto my zealous *Muse*,
> What kinde of creature I could most desire,
>   To honor, serve, and love; as *Poets* use.
> I meant to make her faire, and free, and wise,
>   Of greatest bloud, and yet more good then great;
> I meant the day-starre should not brighter rise,
>   Nor lend like influence from his lucent seat.
> I meant shee should be curteous, facile, sweet,
>   Hating that solemne vice of greatnesse, pride;
> I meant each softest vertue, there should meet,
>   Fit in that softer bosome to reside.
> Onely a learned, and a manly soule
>   I purpos'd her; that should, with even powers,
> The rock, the spindle, and the sheeres controule
>   Of destinie, and spin her owne free houres.
> Such when I meant to faine, and wish'd to see,
>   My *Muse* bad, *Bedford* write, and that was shee.

Many of the collection's ideas gather and echo here. The dedication's Cerberus of "riot, pride, and self-love" is tamed by one "faire, and free, and wise"; "curteous, facile, sweet"; perfect in nature, behavior and spirit; and one who inspires the poet to "honor, serve, and love." Here at last is one, unlike Cecil, who fully enacts the proper relation between "goodness" and

---

73. For an "anxious" reading of these poems, see Roger B. Rollin, "The Anxiety of Identification: Jonson and the Rival Poets," 139–42.

"greatness" while avoiding its great danger, pride. Here too is the "manliness" which the poet feared for in "To My Muse." Here, finally, is a "soule" that with "even powers" can overcome the power of the fates, "controule" its own destinie, and "spin [its] owne free houres." The most perfect flower of the civilizing effort made in the *Epigrammes* is freedom, the free exercise of the personality, the "true self-love" described by Vives that has been from the outset the purpose of the weeding and watering, by custom and contract, of nature in men.[74] How well Jonson did to describe her (or the idea of her) as

> LUCY, you brightnesse of our spheare, who are
> The *Muses* evening, as their morning-starre.
> (XCIV.15–16)

She is one who can transform change into pattern, rhythm, music.

"Inviting a Friend to Supper" (CI), a literal "symposium," shows us this ideal brought home in the free exercise of the speaker's personality as both poet and man. It immediately precedes the epigram to Pembroke, providing a banquet for those who will, in the next poem, be found together in battle. It presents the fullest expression of the communion of the like-minded, those who keep "faith." Yet what is most remarkable about the poem is the transformation it enacts in the relation of speaker and hearer, poet and audience:

> To night, grave sir, both my poore house, and I
> Doe equally desire your companie:
> Not that we thinke us worthy such a ghest,
> But that your worth will dignifie our feast,
> With those that come; whose grace may make that seeme
> Something, which, else, could hope for no esteeme.
> (1–6)

How conscious the speaker is ("my poore house, and I") of himself and of his social inferiority to the "grave sir" so elaborately flattered. How will it be possible to reach the "innocent liberty" of equals that they enjoy at the end? There is, of course, the shared pleasure in the contemplation of the likely (and unlikely) viands, but the effective cause of the changed relation is the speaker's own disingenuous self-mockery in admitting to social climb-

---

74. Raymond Southall observes that in Jonson "the desired end . . . is not . . . high formality and rigidity . . . [but] ease and negligence . . . simplicity, freedom" ("Understanding Jonson," 87).

ing and vanity as a poet. Gone now are the anxieties of "To My Muse"; gone too is the greedy feverishness of the "famisht" Narcissus who could rack "the wide world's store" and of Volpone's invitation to Celia to eat the phoenix itself. Here the richness and variety of forms is celebrated without the anxiety (and without the means!) to possess them. Instead, the speaker takes a measured delight in the multiplicity of nature, of experience, and of himself. This speaker, the perfected "Jonson," can describe the imagined banquet with both exuberance and self-control, pleasure reconciled to virtue, where men may "speake their mindes, amidst their meate"—the spirit and the flesh in a free comity made possible by self-knowledge and the sense of contract. These create the invitation perfect and make possible the heroic vision of civilized men and women in civilized association that the *Epigrammes* were written to serve:

> Nor shall our cups make any guiltie men:
> But, at our parting, we will be, as when
> We innocently met. No simple word,
> That shall be utter'd at our mirthfull boord,
> Shall make us sad next morning: or affright
> The libertie, that wee'll enjoy to night.
>
> (37-42)

No consideration of the *Epigrammes* as a "book" can ignore the apparently anomalous final epigram (CXXXIII), containing "On the Famous Voyage" and "The Voyage it Selfe." Being nearly five times as long as any of the others and much longer than any of Martial's and being a "narration," it appears to contradict Jonson's own criteria for the epigram. Its subject and manner set Swinburne to talking about "Parisian cesspool divers" and opining that "coprology should be left to Frenchmen."[75] Moreover, the poem seems deliberately to spoil or to challenge the positive "masque" element that predominates in the second half, thereby undermining the book's intent and effect as I have described it. Is it, as Swinburne and others have thought, simply a mistake? A lapse of taste, or judgment, or both? If not, what is it doing here?

Three things seem clear. First, despite a steady undercurrent of low satire represented late in the collection by such poems as "On Groyne" (CXVII), "On Gut" (CXVIII), and "To Mime" (CXXIX), this poem contrasts sharply in tone and mood with those that immediately precede it, even as in form it contrasts with all the other epigrams. It acts, therefore, as a

---

75. Swinburne, *A Study of Ben Jonson*, 95.

"turn" for the book, giving to the collection as a whole a structure of exposition and conclusion similar to that found in each of the poems. Second, as a turn, comment, or judgment on the collection, it necessarily contains frequent reminiscences, inversions, and allusions to elements in earlier poems.[76] Third, being cast as a mock-epic, it retrospectively establishes and comments upon the "epic" ambitions of all that has gone before.

What kind of comment is it and to what end? The heroic moral life depicted in the *Epigrammes* will be validated by satirizing false and therefore "vulgar" ideas of heroism, civilization, progress, and the "modern" world. Thus, we have a false epic journey, the "brave adventure of two wights" who undertook, so far as the "action" goes, to row up the Thames, depicted at length as an open sewer, to a brothel in Holborne, where discovering that "great PROSERPINA, / Is now from home" (180-81), they took several "judges" "to witnesse of their action: / And so went bravely backe, without protraction" (191-92). Sardonic reference is made to several classical and modern epics, the main analogy to Aeneas' journey to "Hell" being made explicit at several points. Equally useful is the adoption of a false or ironic narrator who loudly disparages classical heroism and the classical epic while proclaiming the superiority of the present:

> No more let *Greece* her bolder fables tell
> Of HERCULES, or THESEUS going to *hell*,
> ORPHEUS, ULYSSES: or the *Latine Muse*,
> With tales of *Troyes* just knight, our faiths abuse:
> We have a SHELTON, and a HEYDEN got,
> Had power to act, what they to faine had not.
> All, that they boast of STYX, of ACHERON,
> COCYTUS, PHLEGETON, our have prov'd in one;
> The filth, stench, noyse: save only what was there
> Subtly distinguish'd, was confused here.
>
> (1-10)

One could scarcely imagine a more direct inversion of the humanistic "faith" and "piety" extolled earlier than this blast of ignorance and self-

---

76. We may note, for example, such things as the comments on heroic voyaging (ll. 1-20) vs. the epigrams to Sir John (XXXII) and William Roe (CXXVIII); as well as the references to alchemy (ll. 93-97 vs. Epigram VI); to bawds (*passim*); to "Pythagoras" and the metempsychosis of "Bankes the juggler" (ll. 155 ff. vs. Epigram XCV); and all the noisome effluvia of the body, earlier held in check. See also van den Berg's fine discussion of the poem (*Action*, 103-8), which also sees it as a parody of the "main action of the epigrams" that "throw[s] into high relief the techniques of [Jonson's] serious poetry" (105).

importance that slops together in "confusion" all the strands, all the rivers, all the names of the past which the speaker throughout has been so concerned to distinguish "subtly."⁷⁷ The prologue concludes:

> Then let the former age, with this content her,
> Shee brought the *Poets* forth, but ours th'adventer.
>
> (19–20)

How Jonson hated the superior modern "man of action" who neither loves nor learns from the past, who does not know that only the poet can deliver the saving vision of a golden world, and who sits immersed in self-satisfaction, playing like a child with its own excrement.

The objects of the satire are many.⁷⁸ First is the self-satisfied ignorance that dismisses the past without troubling to understand it. But beyond this are lesser satires on conventional expectations of epic style and action that equate heroism with a certain language or set of mannerisms, Spenserian or otherwise. There is satire on the tendency, visible in the contemporary phenomenon of the "nine days wonder," to mistake eccentricity and publicity for morally significant action—which is rarely dramatic and sometimes scarcely even visible except to the discerning eye of the poet. Finally and most intimately, there is satire on the ineluctable hubris ("that solemne vice of greatnesse, pride") that threatens to contaminate any attempt at heroic action, including that shown in the *Epigrammes*. Those who would practice the moral heroism here demonstrated need the mock-heroic to maintain a sane self-knowledge. As in "To My Muse," in which the poet regains his authority by recognizing its limits, so now the book will gain its "authority" as the reader recognizes its limits—and his own.⁷⁹ Like Justice

---

77. Cf. Peterson's discussion of the blending and distinguishing of epic strands in CXVIII (*Imitation and Praise*, 33–43).

78. See Peter E. Medine's instructive "Object and Intent in Jonson's 'Famous Voyage'" for identifications of contemporary allusions and for the conclusion that Jonson intended both a general satire on the decay of learning and manners, and a parodic shot at Harington's "narrations."

79. On the necessary failure of the epic collection to achieve "absolute authority," see Victor P. H. Li, "The Vanity of Length: The Long Poem as Problem in Pound's *Cantos* and Williams' *Paterson*," 13. Maus observes that "as Jonson's career progresses, his comic trials become more and more ironic, instead of displaying the authority of his judges, they show up their weaknesses" (*Roman Frame of Mind*, 128)—with the result that the burden is shifted to the reader. Cf. A. Bartlett Giamatti, *Exile and Change in Renaissance Literature*, 10: "Renaissance epics often teach us not to trust Renaissance epics. They force us back toward life, civic and active; they urge us to learn, by reading, how to live—not how to substitute books for the world."

Adam Overdo in *Bartholmew Fayre,* who had sought to root out all "enormities," author and reader must at the end "remember you are but *Adam,* Flesh and blood! you have your frailty, forget your other name of *Overdoo,* and invite us all to supper" (V.vi.96-98). A certain stink of humanity remains. Does it undermine the "better world" the speaker has been building? I think rather that it is intended, through a humbling self-acknowledgement, to make it possible. Just as "To My Muse" provides at the center of the book a validating crisis for the poet, so the "Famous Voyage" at the end is a validating crisis for the reader and for the whole enterprise. Only those who acknowledge their "frailty," who give up the infantile egotism embodied in this excremental vision, who try to live heroically without mistaking themselves for heroes, will have overcome "riot, pride, and self-love," earned their "supper"—and understood this book.

* * *

Jonson conceived of the epigram, and more particularly of the epigram collection or "book," as a vehicle for heroic poetry, the highest reach of a poet's ambition, and his *Epigrammes* largely fulfill that ambition. Like experience itself, the form is intense, fragmentary, complicated, and confused in its rhythms and counter-rhythms; yet it is so united by continuities in conception, method, and purpose that we sense, in Hegel's words, "a reality that has been grasped in its substance and lived through." Again one thinks of Montaigne for comparable range and vitality, though Jonson's purpose is clearer and his effects more concentrated.

Important as they are in themselves, the *Epigrammes* also play a significant role in the Jonson canon. How far we have come from *Cynthias Revels*—not in terms of moral insight (this is much of a piece throughout), but in Jonson's understanding of the artistic implications of his peculiar moral vision.[80] In *Cynthias Revels,* he divided his material into the mythic, the stories that tell the eternal truths, and the empiric, the application of those truths to experience, and he then treated those materials in accor-

---

80. Criticism that seeks to explain changes in Jonson's work by inferring some evolution in his moral outlook or purpose—whether from authoritarianism to tolerance, or from didacticism to despair—seems to me often unpersuasive on two counts: it relies too heavily on a debatable interpretation of a single work (*Bartholmew Fayre*) that Jonson did not trouble to include in the Folio of 1616; and it neglects the primacy of his artistic concerns. Jonson is, I think, best seen as a self-conscious, self-created literary artist whose representational choices in the plays and poems (the treatment of authority figures within the plays, the relation of audience to spectacle, and so on) are most simply explained as part of his evolving mastery of his art. He changes his tactics more often than his mind.

dance with a simple notion of literary decorum: the more "significant" the matter, the more elaborate and rarefied its presentation. Taken together, *Volpone* and the *Epigrammes* reveal the increasing sophistication of Jonson's art. No longer do we find the crude assumption that high seriousness demands poetry, lesser seriousness only drama.[81] Instead, a single dramatic "poem" like *Volpone* fuses the mythic and the empiric, the morality play and the city comedy into an interinanimating whole. A single poetic collection like the *Epigrammes* juxtaposes the highest ideals with the most squalid realities. What makes these things possible? With regard to drama, Jonson appears to have discovered two things: first, that plot is indeed its soul; second, that in his vision of a fallen world, all plots are finally tragic, though they may be used to foster a comic self-awareness. Thus, instead of the aesthetic confusions of the early plays (Are they to be fully dramatic, or partly narrative? Is the author, or his representative, to appear in them, or only through them?), *Volpone* and the *Epigrammes* show him in full command of means as well as ends. Also clearer is the relation between dramatic and nondramatic form. All the comedies have tragedy at their back, a tragic sense that gives them weight and tone, even as Rembrandt's dark backgrounds enrich the lightest subjects. The best that may be hoped is that the downward spiral, the tragic rhythms of frenzied metamorphosis, dissolution, or death may be arrested for a moment's amused judgment, a moment's comedy. The *Epigrammes* form a collection of such moments.

Consider in this connection the inevitable comparison with Shakespeare, in particular the artist figures each writer created late in his career: Prospero in *The Tempest,* educing and protecting the golden possibilities of love and forgiveness despite the long, brassy usurpation of cynicism abetted by weakness; Compass in *The Magnetic Lady,* a mathematical "limiter," hoping only to hold the disparate elements together for a few hours (and a supper) before they fall back into inevitable chaos.[82] Although neither is coterminous with his creator, they point to essential differences. Jonson's is a world of intractable darkness, in which man attempts to celebrate and

---

81. This assumption persists, however, in some of Jonson's readers. See, for example, J. B. Bamborough, *Ben Jonson,* ch. 1.

82. See Compass's first speech:

> As if I can but hold them all together,
> And draw 'hem to a sufferance of themselves,
> But till the Dissolution of the Dinner;
> I shall have just occasion to beleeve
> My wit is magisteriall; and our selves
> Take infinite delight, i'the successe.
>
> (I.i.9–14)

maximize those bright moments of awareness, judgment, and understanding (Volpone, quoting Catullus, says to Celia, "But if once we lose this light / 'Tis, with us, perpetuall night"). Shakespeare's is a world at once darker and lighter, suffused with mystery rather than misunderstanding, in which man is beset by an actual and potential evil that goes beyond even the insatiable desires of the narcissistic ego but is also aided by an equally intractable (or inexhaustible) good.

Comparison with Milton is also instructive. Like Jonson, Milton, in seeking adequate form for the presentation of his whole vision, debated between drama and narrative. Also like Jonson, he faced the artistic difficulty that evil is, to an audience of fallen creatures, more immediately interesting, sympathetic, and vivid than good.[83] Yet neither will "write things false, nor hide things true" and must therefore give us both heaven and hell, the domains of virtue and vice, each with its characteristic rhythms, beauties, triumphs, fates. Jonson, while able to combine these in a single work, is not able to make them part of a single plot. He lacks, perhaps, Milton's faith, his supreme capacity for synthesis, his ability to demonstrate the ways in which evil not only destroys itself, but also serves the purposes of good—to justify the paradoxical ways of god to man.

The full representation of Jonson's vision of the good still possible, the response one can make to the conditions presented in the plays, demands on the contrary the plotless form of the poetic collection, a collection of discrete responses. And these responses must adapt themselves, even as the speaker of the *Epigrammes* does, to the shifting initiatives of nature in a continuing hand-to-hand, poem-by-poem confrontation, "*actus contra actum*," of epic significance.[84] Although in *Volpone* a providential ironic economy insures that evil will, given enough time, necessarily destroy itself, nothing within the play adequately confronts the natural dynamism of self-love. But in their analysis of the economy of change and contract, of the possibility of meeting and mastering change in concert with others by means of contracts—piety, faith, friendship—the *Epigrammes* propose an answer to the problem of self-love and prepare the way for the still larger consideration of the possibilities for moral and social life in the later poetry.

In the *Epigrammes* Jonson comes as close as he ever does to the "proper

---

83. Summers observes that "Jonson attempted one of the most difficult things a poet can conceive in any age: to present an ideal of the mean, of rational control and fulfilled public function, so that it seizes the imagination of the reader and stirs his emotions" (*The Heirs of Donne and Jonson*, 34).

84. See Maus, *Roman Frame of Mind*, 150, on Jonson's "increasing awareness that the Roman moralists' conception of virtue resists dramatization."

embattling" of vice and virtue that he thought the primary obligation of the poet.[85] The method is, of course, juxtaposition rather than synthesis, leading to affirmations that are, taken as a whole, partial and suggestive (all now depends upon the reader, who must both understand and act upon his understanding) rather than resounding and unequivocal. Yet it remains the most complete of his works, the one in which he most clearly demonstrates his claim to be the public poet, master of the permutations of change and passion, master also of the personal and cultural responses to them. As physician to the body of humanity, he understands man's divided condition but can make from that "division" healing music. In epigram XXI, he says (albeit ironically): "The bodies stripes, I see, the soule may save." He takes in hand both the coarse and the fine material of human life, convinced that its moral "diseases" can be purged and mortified only through self-knowledge and self-judgment, that its ever-threatened health and civility can be maintained only through continually fulfilled, continually renewed contracts with the self and with others. Here we are close to the center of Jonson's vision. As Douglas Bush has remarked, "Jonson the playwright and even Jonson the lyrist may be said to see and think and feel in terms of the epigram."[86] Other of his works are perhaps more perfect; none is more complete or more fully realized. In their peculiar way, the *Epigrammes* are indeed the "ripest of [his] studies," comprising in form, subject, and fulfillment of his poetic vocation the fullest statement he has given us of his vision of "humanitie," its limitations and possibilities, a statement upon which he is willing to be judged.

85. H&S, 8:595.
86. Douglas Bush, *English Literature in the Earlier Seventeenth Century*, 109.

Chapter IV

The Subtlest Maze of All

It may seem paradoxical to say that Jonson is one of our greatest poets of love. Yet he is that rare creature, a love poet who is not also a romantic poet, a Dante without a Beatrice, one who questions, sometimes playfully, sometimes angrily, not only the proximate conventions of the Petrarchan sonneteers, but the whole shift in sensibility that C. S. Lewis describes in *The Allegory of Love*. Lewis argues that the confluence of late classical and medieval Christian ideas with the feudal social system of western Europe produced a new idea (visible in Dante, Petrarch, Castiglione, and Spenser), a new value placed on romantic love and even on sensual desire.[1] It is, in the words of Pietro Bembo in *The Courtier*, "the lowest rung of the ladder by which we can ascend to true love," that is, the love of God.[2] Jonson often seems to share this Platonizing view, particularly in the masques, where it plays a prominent part, but also, as we have seen, in such an early play as *Cynthias Revels*.

But Jonson's attitude to received ideas is ever critical, and he criticizes the established consensus on the significance of romantic love at its most vulnerable point, the division allegorically figured in the combat of Eros and Anteros: love as it affects the body, the passions, the will, the self in search of gratification versus love as it affects the mind, the soul, the self in search of perfection. Unlike the sonneteers who present these elements as a continuum, however complex or retrograde, Jonson is always more inclined to see them as a dialectical opposition.[3] Thus we find the simple opposi-

---

1. C. S. Lewis, *The Allegory of Love*, ch. 1.
2. Baldesar Castiglione, *The Book of the Courtier*, 328.
3. Maus writes of Jonson's "suspicion of the sublimatory process" (*Roman Frame of Mind*, 89) and the "selective materialism" of the Roman moralists, who, "when virtue rather than vice is under consideration," "tend to conceive of the body not as the mind's expressive vehicle, but as its antagonist" (28). See also Lawrence Venuti, "Why Jonson Wrote Not of Love."

tions in *Cynthias Revels,* or between Volpone and Celia, or Celia and her husband Corvino: one side all heavenly self-sacrifice, the other all earthly self-gratification. The examination of love in the nondramatic poetry, particularly in *The Forrest,* is more complex and interesting; it presents Jonson's most considered and most satisfactory response to the problem of human nature that preoccupied him early and late, that of self-love. In the *Workes* of 1616, *The Forrest* simply follows the *Epigrammes* without a new dedication, and indeed these poems take up where the *Epigrammes* leave off and build upon the civilizing basis of contract and judgment established in the first collection. The *Epigrammes* present a way to restrain the "body," helping it to keep "shape" and maintain "faith"; *The Forrest* examines the ways in which it may be made fruitful. Once self-love has been restrained, the growth of true love, in body and in soul, may begin. This "action" will not be simple, no more than that of the *Epigrammes,* for as Jonson's Daedalus, the artificer in *Pleasure Reconcild to Vertue* (1618) observes, "all actions of mankind / are but a Laborinth, or maze," and now we "are to prove / the subtlest maze of all: that's *Love*" (261–62, 299–300).

* * *

Like the *Epigrammes, The Forrest* as a whole has suffered from the brilliant success of some of its parts. "Drinke to me, onely" (IX) is among the most frequently anthologized poems in the language, and the other two songs to Celia, "Come my Celia" (V) and "Kisse me, sweet" (VI), are not far behind. "To Penshurst" (II) (with or without "To Sir Robert Wroth" [III]) is the most frequently studied and commented upon of Jonson's poems, as often for it politics as for its poetry.[4] "To Heaven" has been admired for its "tough-minded" religious sincerity.[5] Other poems have provided material for those studying the history of the ode (XIV) or the verse epistle (XII, XIII). "Why I write not of Love" (I) has been analyzed as a contribution to the debate over the adequacy of poetry and poetic convention, or of language itself, to represent complex experience.[6]

The neglect of the collection has been natural enough, for its most

---

4. See, for example, Raymond Southall, *Literature and the Rise of Capitalism,* 95–105, for the conservative view. Raymond Williams, on the other side, finds in the poem "not country life but social compliment; the familiar hyperboles of the aristocracy and its attendants" (*The Country and the City,* 33).

5. See Kerrigan, "Shame and Scorn."

6. See Anne Ferry, *All in War with Time: Love Poetry of Shakespeare, Donne, Jonson, and Marvell,* ch. 3; also Murray Krieger, *Theory of Criticism: A Tradition and Its System,* 233–37.

striking feature is its immense variety. Whatever else it may be, it is a virtuoso display of Jonson's mastery of classic and contemporary forms: song, epistle, ode, epode, complaint, psalm, satire, as well as hybrids of his own breeding. He displays a corresponding mastery of moods and voices: men and a woman; young, old, middle-aged; confident, joyful, despairing, lonely, avuncular, angry, fair-minded, proud, humble. Rather than the intensive art of the *Epigrammes* (nearly all in heroic couplets), here we find ten different metric patterns within fifteen poems, providing a banquet of poetry with a menu as exquisite and varied as any Jonson's would-be gourmands could have imagined.[7] To describe and to estimate the variety and the unity of a collection such as *The Forrest* poses delicate problems of critical tact, problems complicated from the beginning by Jonson's rather too helpful preface to the *Under-wood,* first published posthumously in 1640, in which he says that "With the same leave, the Ancients call'd that kind of body *Sylva,* or "Υλη, in which there were workes of divers nature, and matter congested; as the multitude call Timber-trees, promiscuously growing, a *Wood,* or *Forrest.*"[8] Although the description is conventional, it points to the most important sources of variety: "divers nature," the many verse kinds; "matter congested," the differences in subject, speaker, and treatment; "promiscuously growing," written for different people, occasions, and reasons, and not originally intended to be read together. Yet the collection seems, as others have observed, to be more than a miscellaneous sampler, however impressive.[9] If this is a "forest," it still possesses unities "of soyle, of ayre, of wood, of water" and it is clearly a specimen forest. The growth of the poems may have been "promiscuous"; their selection and arrangement was not. Finally, like a forest, it is a place of mystery, perhaps of danger, where the roots drive deeper and last longer than in field or garden, where one must hunt for one's food and (as in Shakespeare's forests) for oneself.

7. There are pentameter couplets (II, XII, XIII, XV); tetrameter couplets (I, V, VI); pentameter/tetrameter couplets (III); pentameter/trimeter couplets (XI); a pentameter terzain (X); trochaic tetrameter couplets (VIII); a tetrameter quatrain (IV); a tetrameter quatrain and couplet stanza (VII); an eight-line interwoven tetrameter stanza (IX); and a complex ten-line stanza with lines of varying lengths (XIV).

8. Herford and Simpson note that this is Jonson's translation of "a quotation from Caspar Gavartius' commentaries on Statius, 1616, explaining the title *Sylvae* for Statius' lyrics" (H&S 8:577–78). Jonson used the quotation itself to preface *Timber*.

9. See Graham Bradshaw, "Three Poems Ben Jonson did not Write: A Note on Jonson's Christian Humanism," and Jonathan Z. Kamholtz, "Ben Jonson's Green World: Structure and Imaginative Unity in *The Forrest.*"

Statius, evidently the classical model for the Renaissance use of the term, shows in his *Sylvae* just the "divers, congested, and promiscuous" qualities Jonson mentions, as in rambling, headlong fashion he addresses wife, friends, and emperor, meditates on statues, trees, villas, parrots, temples, roads, sleep; celebrates birthdays and weddings; laments his father's death. He presents this material in a heterogeneous (and supposedly unpremeditated), rhapsodic mixture of natural description, epideictic address, mythological parallel, sober reflection, and expressions of fear, desire, and hope.[10] Through this method he achieves a variety of striking effects and often succeeds in uniting humble observations and high aspirations in a way occasionally reminiscent of Jonson.

Despite the variety and heterogeneity of *The Forrest,* the impression it makes is, on the whole, very different from that of Statius' studied effusions. However tempting Jonson's note on *Sylvae* may seem, I believe the significant model to be not Statius but Jonson's favorite Roman, Horace.[11] I will argue that in *The Forrest* Jonson is not only "Horatian" in some general sense, but is consciously imitating Horace's *Odes,* Book IV; that *The Forrest* possesses a subtle unity; and that, again like Horace's fourth book, it develops possibilities only suggested in the earlier poetry, specifically the *Epigrammes*.

Jonson's general debt to Horace is well known. He is without question the predecessor in poetry Jonson most often translated, imitated, and alluded to. Jonson translated the entire *Ars Poetica,* and adopted many of its precepts in his own critical thinking. He closely translated two of the *Odes* (3.9 and 4.1) and the second Epode ("*Beatus ille*"); he freely translated a satire (2.1) for use as Act III, scene v, of *Poetaster*. Moreover, Jonson cast himself as Horace in *Poetaster,* described himself "as Horace Fat," delivered "A Speech according to Horace" (*Under-wood,* XLII, XLIV), and was pleased to be regarded as the "English Horace." All this testifies to Jonson's abiding admiration for and complete familiarity with Horace's work and his continuing desire to "english" him in art and life. That Jonson was incompletely successful in adapting the style of the delicate, gracious,

---

10. Both Ann Jacobson Lauinger ("The *Sylva* and Civilizing Form in Ben Jonson's *The Forrest* and *The Under-wood,*" Ph.D. diss.) and Alastair Fowler ("The Silva Tradition and Jonson's *The Forrest*") have attempted to establish a Renaissance "Sylva" tradition in which to read the collection. But the "tradition" remains rather loose, as does Jonson's relation to it.

11. For a general argument that *The Forrest* was conceived as "an extensive imitation of the forms and temper of Horatian poetry," see van den Berg, *Action,* ch. 5.

amused, and melancholy Horace to his own sterner temper has often been observed. Yet in *The Forrest* he comes close enough that both affinities and divergences emerge with unusual clarity.

Horace's first three books of *Odes* were published together in 23 B.C. and established his reputation as a lyric poet.[12] The fourth book, appearing ten years later, acts as both culmination of and comment upon the earlier collection. It is much briefer (containing fifteen poems, while the others have thirty-eight, twenty, and thirty), yet within its short compass, Horace employs several stanzaic forms, eight different metric patterns (one of them uniquely), and ranges from eight lines to seventy-six. There is a corresponding variety of subjects, moods, and rhetorical devices: he addresses Venus, Apollo, his Muse, his patron Maecenas, other poets, Augustus and members of the Claudian family; he speaks of war and peace, beauty and decay, birthdays, spring, love, old age, and poetry. Despite this variety, it possesses a "careful articulation"[13] and "refinement" (of arrangement) that sets it apart from all the other poetic "books" of its period.[14]

This impression of unity is easier to feel than to account for. The commonest approach has been to search for structural symmetries in the arrangement of the book, to choose, for example, the "central" poem (4.8) and argue that its position and subject matter—the special nature and force of poetry among human activities, to bring the dead to life, to preserve the past, to raise passing suffering into imperishable myth—make it a radiating center for the entire book. Or one can look at the first and last poems, noticing that the first begins with the "cruel" Venus who keeps the poet in endless turmoil and the last concludes with the "kind" Venus, mother of the Rome that Augustus makes peaceful and fruitful, and argue that the polarities of public and private life, civility and unrest, and their enigmatic combination in the person of Venus are the book's informing concerns. It is a subtle book and makes its effects subtly. Indeed, although modern critics agree that it is the most unified book of the *Odes,* they are in considerably less agreement over just what constitutes its unity of effect and intent.

---

12. On Odes I-III, see Santirocco, *Unity and Design in Horace's Odes*. More generally, I have found useful Eduard Fraenkel, *Horace*; N. E. Collinge, *The Structure of Horace's Odes*; Steele Commager, *The Odes of Horace: A Critical Study*; L. P. Wilkinson, *Horace and His Lyric Poetry*; Jacques Perret, *Horace*; and the translations and commentary of C. E. Bennett (*Horace: The Odes and Epodes*) and Joseph P. Clancy (*The Odes and Epodes of Horace: A Modern English Verse Translation*).
13. Collinge, *The Structure of Horace's Odes*, 42.
14. Fraenkel, *Horace*, 410.

Difficulty in interpretation arises from Horace's most characteristic strengths as an artist, his use of a "mosaic" technique and of a rhythm that has been described as "appearance, disappearance, and return."[15] The analogy to mosaic composition has been particularly fruitful for the understanding of Horace's technique both in writing poems and in collecting them into books. The application of this idea to his handling of syntax and word order is clear, for Horace takes maximum advantage of the opportunities an inflected language presents for artful derangement of "natural" word order, placement of substantive and modifier, etc., to produce the effect memorably described by Nietzsche as a "mosaic of words, in which every word by sound, by position, and by meaning diffuses its influence to right and left and over the whole; the minimum in compass and number of symbols, the maximum achieved in the effectiveness of those symbols."[16] A similar principle seems to underlie the arrangement of the poems into books, but as we have no grammar of "interpoetic" syntax, its application is more problematic. One speaks of juxtaposition, contrast, recurrence, complementarity, and so on, but it is hard to attain a sense of the whole. Difficult though it is to generalize confidently about the overall pattern (N. E. Collinge warns that "it is folly to think that even most of the *Odes* are grouped according to some master plan"),[17] it is I think possible to speak with some confidence of the effect on the reader. Collinge remarks that "what really happens, if Horace speaks of the same thing, more or less, in a close sequence of odes, is that the reader's mind is held in a certain receptive poise rather than fixed in a logical groove."[18]

What then does a reader, poised and receptive, receive in Book Four? A full analysis is beyond the scope of this study, but we may begin by

---

15. Clancy discusses both techniques (*Odes and Epodes of Horace*, 13–21). Santirocco discerns three principles at work: "*Variatio* . . . prevents the reader from becoming bored; static patterns enliven the whole through surface artifice; and dynamic sequences create momentum and, at last, a sense of closure" (*Unity and Design in Horace's Odes*, 174).

16. Nietzsche, *Werke*, 6:3.149: "Dies Mosaik von Worten, wo jedes Wort als Klang, als Ort, als Begriff, nach rechts und links und ueber das Ganze hin seine Kraft ausstroemt, dies minimum in Umfang und Zahl der Zeichen, dies damit erzielte maximum in der Energie der Zeichen." The translation is Wilkinson's (*Horace and His Lyric Poetry*, 4).

17. Collinge, *The Structure of Horace's Odes*, 52. William S. Anderson has recently concluded that "no Roman poet of the Augustan era composed his book on principles of mathematical symmetry" ("The Theory and Practice of Poetic Arrangement From Vergil to Ovid," in *Poems in Their Place*, ed. Fraistat, 56).

18. Collinge, *The Structure of Horace's Odes*, 41. The effect Collinge calls "responsion" (ch. 3) in Horace is similar to William V. Spanos's idea of "resonance" in Jonson ("The Real Toad in the Jonsonian Garden," 6).

observing that it is a "later" book that corrects, amplifies, or deepens its larger predecessor. Horace had ended Book III with grand finality:

> My memorial is done: it will outlast bronze,
> it is taller than the Pyramids' royal mounds,
> and no rain and corrosion, no raging Northwind
> can tear it down, nor the innumerable years
> in succession, and the transitory ages.
> I will not wholly die: the greater part of me
> shall escape the goddess of death: I will grow on,
> kept alive by posterity's praise. As long as
> high priest and silent virgin climb the Capitol,
> I will be known where the wild Aufidus thunders,
> in the land where water is scarce, whose farmers
> Daunus once ruled, a man who rose from poverty,
> who led the way, adapting Aeolian song
> to Italian verses. Accept the high honors
> I have won by your kindness, and graciously crown
> my hair, Melpomene, with Apollo's laurel.[19]
>
> (3.30)

What more is there to say? He has accomplished his purposes as a man and a poet, raised himself from poverty and obscurity through the power of his poetry to a kind of heroism and immortality "kept alive by posterity's praise." It is the perfected victory of energy, intelligence, and urbanity over unfavorable circumstances, the successful adaptation of Greek models to Roman purposes, a complete victory for both the man and his culture. This is the proper, the inevitable ending of the "story" implicit throughout the first three books. Early on he had announced his character and program when he demurred from writing the praises of a general, Agrippa:

> to tell of these things,
> or the dread peeve of Achilles, who never knew
> how to give in, or clever Ulysses' sea voyage,
> or the cruel house of Atreus,
> I do not try: major themes, minor poet;
> propriety and the non-belligerent Muse
> forbid me to spoil Caesar's praises and yours
> with a botched-up job.
>
> What poet is worthy to write of Mars in his armor

---

19. I use Clancy's translations throughout.

> of adamant, or Meriones, blackened
> with Trojan dust, or Diomed, aided by Athena,
> > in whom gods met their match?
>
> I am a poet of parties, battles of virgins
> valiantly fighting off boys with their manicured nails
> I celebrate, my heart at ease or on fire,
> > in my usual featherbrained way.
>
> > > (1.6.2–5)

    The poem is typical both for what it says and what it does. Horace declines the major themes, heroic and tragic, happy in his role of "minor poet," cultivating his perceptions of civilized life, political gossip, the wars of love, and his shifting self. Unashamed and at peace with his limits, he extricates himself from an awkward and unwelcome situation with such graceful, urbane self-deprecation that Agrippa may not, for the moment, notice that he is being brushed off. This sort of urbanity, a "receptive poise" of mind and character, is the quality repeatedly tested and repeatedly achieved throughout the first three books as the poet confronts the full range of social and personal experiences, and its victory is triumphantly celebrated in the last poem.

    This makes rather an imposing background for Book IV. With so much accomplished, why is another book necessary at all? How can he escape anticlimax? What strikes one immediately is that the fundamental tone has changed. The first poem begins:

> Those wars, Venus, are long over,
> > and now you provoke them again. Please, please,
> > > spare me.
> I am not what I was when dear
> > Cinara ruled me. Put an end to your efforts,
> cruel mother of sweet Cupids,
> > to soften the stiffness of a man now fifty
> by your gentle orders: go where
> > the young men invite you with flattering prayers.
>
> > > (4.1.1–2)

He is older and feels even older than he is. The easy confidence with which he had, for example, once invoked Venus to whip the arrogant Chloe (3.26) has given way to an anxious (and unsuccessful) plea for his own peace of mind. But now he cannot handle things so easily: Venus comes and goes (and comes again) as she wills. The first three books tested and affirmed the power of urbanity; this final book explores its limits, as Horace encounters not so much social or personal problems, but the intractable primary realities that even the greatest urbanity and civility cannot master. One senses throughout an ardent desire to press to the roots of experience, to identify and to acknowledge the fundamental forces that must have their way, whether one will or no. These forces take many forms throughout the book, as they continually appear, disappear, and (hauntingly) return, but may be reduced to two main principles: the multifarious, enigmatic power of love and the ineluctable power of age and death.

In the face of realities too large and powerful for any one man, however poised, to master, Horace turns to those cultural devices which, like poetry and the family, are at once private and public. Poetry is essential because it alone can preserve whatever is valuable in human life; only the Muse "forbids a praiseworthy man to perish" (4.8). It is also important to the poet himself because poetry enables him to represent and do justice to those parts of experience that he cannot master: "bitter sorrows will grow milder with music" (4.11.9). His concern with the family, particularly with that of Augustus and the Claudians, requires more explanation. His interest is practical, in that these people are the political and military bulwark of the peace and civility enjoyed by the state. But as a family they also exemplify, as no individual could, the successful encounter with love and time: Venus made fruitful in the nurturing of children, and the vicarious immortality of perpetual succession. This is the final vision with which Horace comforts himself at the close of the book:

> All of us, on working days and holy days,
> among the gifts of laughter-loving Bacchus,
> accompanied by wives and children,
>   will first, as is proper, pray to the gods,
>
> then, in the way of our fathers, to the sound
> of Lydian flutes we will hymn our heroes
> and their noble achievements and Troy,
>   Anchises, and kind Venus' descendants.
>   (4.15.7–8)

This represents, like the end of the first three books, a victory of sorts, not so much for Horace, the civilized man, as for civilization itself, which through the leadership of Augustus, accommodates itself to, and wrings a blessing from, the eternal realities to which the individual, however urbane, must finally submit.

* * *

Evidence of several kinds suggests that Jonson had the fourth book of *Odes* specifically in mind when arranging *The Forrest*. There are notable external similarities. Both collections contain fifteen poems chosen to demonstrate a virtuosic mastery of forms and occasions. *The Forrest* is also a "later" collection that builds upon and responds to a larger, "simpler" predecessor, the *Epigrammes*.[20] In the *Workes* of 1616, *The Forrest* follows immediately upon the heels of the *Epigrammes,* and the lack of a separate dedication suggests that it is to be considered along with the earlier collection.

Within the book, several borrowings and structural similarities point to a special connection with *Odes* IV. For example, Jonson's praise of the power of poetry in "Epistle, To Elizabeth Countesse of Rutland" contains a free paraphrase of parts of Horace's 4.8.:

> It is the *Muse,* alone, can raise to heaven,
>   And, at her strong armes end, hold up, and even,
> The soules, shee loves.
>
>   (XII, 41–43)

When Jonson rises to a definition of the good life at the end of "To Sir Robert Wroth," he inserts into a passage imitated from Juvenal a key line taken from *Odes* 4.9. There are obvious analogies between poems concerning the Muse (*Odes,* 4.3 and *Forrest,* X), between those celebrating birthdays (*Odes,* 4.11 and *Forrest,* XIV), and between Horace's beginning with a plea that he escape the power of Venus (and immediately confessing that power) and Jonson's introducing in "Why I write not of Love" a collection of poems that, in its own way, deals with little but love. Similar too is the framing movement in Horace from the "cruel" Venus of the first poem to the "kind" Venus of the last and the movement in Jonson from the initial encounter with Cupid to the final one with God. Moreover, Jonson relies upon members of the Sidney family as the examples, makers, and guarantors of the humane culture he envisions, even as Horace relies upon Augustus and the Claudians.

Both collections represent extended meditations upon and essays into the nature of civility as a public and private necessity, and both explore the accommodations it must make to such primary realities as love and death, good and evil. Further, these meditations complete earlier work (*Odes* 1–3,

---

20. As both the Stationer's Register and Drummond's notes on his reading suggest, the *Epigrammes* may have been published separately in 1612.

The Subtlest Maze of All 101

Epigrammes) that analyzed the more easily handled social and personal challenges to civility.[21] Yet once we have recognized the fundamental similarities of conception and purpose, we can also see the no less significant differences that separate the two poets. Both are poets of "civility" but define the "problem of civility" rather differently. For Horace, it is a matter of perceptions and emotions; for Jonson, a matter of will and activity.

A simple example of these characteristic differences appears in Jonson's translation of *Odes* 4.1:

> Intermissa, Venus, diu
> rursus bella moves. parce, precor, precor.
> non sum qualis eram bonae
>   sub regno Cinarae. desine, dulcium
>
> mater saeva Cupidinum,
>   circa lustra decem flectere mollibus
> iam durum imperiis: abi,
>   quo blandae iuvenum te revocant preces.
>
> tempestivius in domum
>   Pauli, purpureis ales oloribus,
> commisabere Maximi,
>   si torrere iecur quaeris idoneum.
>
> namque et nobilis et decens
>   et pro sollicitis non tacitus reis
> et centum puer artium
>   late signa feret militiae tuae;
>
> et quandoque potentior
>   largi muneribus riserit aemuli,
> Albanos prope te lacus
>   ponet marmoream sub trabe citrea.
>
> illic plurima naribus
>   duces tura lyraeque et Berecyntiae
> delectabere tibiae
>   mixtis carminibus non sine fistula;

---

21. As Kamholtz observes, "the *Epigrammes* and the *Forrest* are complementary groups of poems" ("Ben Jonson's Green World," 174). Kamholtz reads the latter collection as an escape from the former: "Jonson has come to the *Forrest* fleeing the bondage of contractual relationships—social and poetic—because the rational and commercial exchanges that uphold such agreements corrupt both life and art" (171). I think rather that, in Jonson's moral economy, the contracts of the first collection are good in themselves and are the necessary precondition of the freer exchanges and fulfillments of the second.

illic bis pueri die
  numen cum teneris virginibus tuum
laudantes pede candido
  in morem Salium ter quatient humum.

me nec femina nec puer
  iam nec spes animi credula mutui
nec certare iuvat mero
  nec vincire novis tempora floribus.

sed cur heu, Ligurine, cur
  manat rara meas lacrima per genas?
cur facunda parum decoro
  inter verba cadit lingua silentio?

nocturnis ego somniis
  iam captum teneo, iam volucrem sequor
te per gramina Martii
  Campi, te per aquas, dure, volubilis.[22]

> *Venus,* againe thou mov'st a warre
> Long intermitted, pray thee, pray thee spare:
>   I am not such, as in the Reigne
> Of the good *Cynara* I was: Refraine,
>
>   Sower Mother of sweet Loves, forbeare
> To bend a man, now at his fiftieth yeare
>   Too stubborne for Commands so slack:
> Goe where Youths soft intreaties call thee back.
>   More timely hie thee to the house,
> With thy bright Swans, of *Paulus Maximus*:
>   There jest, and feast, make him thine host,
> If a fit livor thou dost seeke to toast;
>   For he's both noble, lovely, young
> And for the troubled Clyent fyl's his tongue,
>   Child of a hundred Arts, and farre
> Will he display the Ensignes of thy warre.
>   And when he smiling finds his Grace
> With thee 'bove all his Rivals gifts take place,
>   He'll thee a Marble Statue make
> Beneath a Sweet-wood Roofe, neere *Alba Lake*:
>   There shall thy dainty Nostrill take
> In many a Gumme, and for thy soft eares sake
>   Shall Verse be set to Harpe and Lute,

---

22. Bennett's text.

> And *Phrygian* Hau'boy, not without the Flute.
>   There twice a day in sacred Laies,
> The Youths and tender Maids shall sing thy praise:
>   And in the *Salian* manner meet
> Thrice 'bout thy Altar with their Ivory feet.
>   Me now, nor Wench, nor wanton Boy,
> Delights, nor credulous hope of mutuall Joy,
>   Nor care I now healths to propound;
> Or with fresh flowers to girt my temple round.
>   But, why, oh why, my *Ligurine*,
> Flow my thin teares, downe these pale cheeks of mine?
>   Or why, my well-grac'd words among,
> With an uncomely silence failes my tongue?
>   Hard-hearted, I dreame every Night
> I hold thee fast! but fled hence, with the Light,
>   Whether in *Mars* his field thou bee,
> Or *Tybers* winding streames, I follow thee.
>   (*Under-wood*, LXXXVI)

So near and yet so far. It is a poor translation: despite occasional felicities, the tone is wrong, the rhetorical situation has been coarsened and distorted, the final stanza misinterpreted, and thereby the chief beauty of the original (the subtle relation between the first eight stanzas and the last two) is lost. In Jonson's version, Venus and the difficulties she poses are essentially external to the speaker and in conflict with him while in the original they are inextricably intertwined with his own personality, putting him in conflict with himself. Thus, for the intimately blended "dulcium mater saeva cupidinum," Jonson gives us the merely paradoxical "Sower Mother of Sweet Loves"; for the "hard," stiff man who wishes (and fears?) to think that he can no longer be "softened," Jonson gives us one who is "Too stubborne for Commands, so slack." A question of competing perceptions has been reduced to a question of competing wills. Similarly, in the suggestion of another victim, Horace's syntax places Venus inside Paulus Maximus ("Pauli, purpureis ales oloribus / comissabere Maximi") while Jonson invents a line that places her firmly outside: "There jest, and feast, make him thine host." In the persuasion that follows, Horace wittily attempts to seduce Venus with her own sensual baits (incense, music, dance) while Jonson merely tries to flatter and cajole her with invented epithets ("*dainty*" Nostrill, "*soft*" eares) and with, of all things, a "Verse" to go with the music. Most marvelous in Horace's poem is the handling of the "appearance, disappearance, return" rhythm, in which Venus challenges the poet and appears by the eighth stanza to have been overcome, the speaker claiming to be beyond the passions, pleasures, and illusions of love. Yet in the last two stanzas he again is plunged head over heels, his voice (and reason) fail him, and he remains between night and dreams ("nocturnis ego somniis")—catching, losing, being caught, first on land, and finally in the unmasterable water. Jonson misunderstands the subtlety of this chastened self-awareness and gratuitously introduces the clumsy "clarification" of "with the Light." This sets up an opposition between sleep and waking which undermines Horace's point that Venus can reduce the mind to a state of helpless ambiguity and helpless dreaming.

How could Jonson have committed this vandalism? Perhaps he did not. He never published the poem; it appears toward the end of the *Under-wood,* where it seems that Jonson's literary executor, Sir Kenelm Digby, is simply piling on whatever stray pieces remain.[23] It may well have been written very early, perhaps even as a school exercise, which would explain Jonson's willingness to make "aquas . . . volubilis" an excuse for a geography lesson on "*Tybers* winding streams." Whatever its provenance, and despite its failings as a translation, it nonetheless points up some of the chief differences between Horace and Jonson. Horace wants to know what things are and how they work; Jonson wants to get things done. Horace excels at depicting the fleeting emotions, ambiguities, velleities, subterranean connections of the mind; Jonson prefers to focus on actions and agents, and the qualities of will and judgment immediately connected with them. These differences are also apparent in *The Forrest,* where Jonson provides an extended meditation on love and what it *does.*

            Why I Write Not of Love

      Some act of *Love*'s bound to reherse,
      I thought to binde him, in my verse:
      Which when he felt, Away (quoth hee)
      Can Poets hope to fetter mee?
      It is enough, they once did get

---

23. How much of the *Under-wood* was arranged by Jonson, what and how strong its unifying intentions were, and to what degree those intentions were ever fulfilled are questions that can never be answered with much confidence. As with the other poetic collections, Herford and Simpson underestimate the unifying impulse. Annabel Patterson's suggestion that the *Under-wood* presents a deliberate "retrospective of his career" ("Lyric and Society," 153) is more plausible, though it perhaps overstates the degree to which this intention is fulfilled.

> MARS, and my *Mother,* in their net:
> I weare not these my wings in vaine.
> With which he fled me: and againe,
> Into my ri'mes could ne're be got
> By any arte. Then wonder not,
> That since, my numbers are so cold,
> When *Love* is fled, and I grow old.

A wry preface for the collection. Indeed, "love" is not only the most common substantive, but in one form or another, his continual concern throughout.[24] What is the source of the obligation described in the first line? Some command by a patron or patroness, like that behind "That Women Are but Mens Shadowes"? Or as Anne Ferry has suggested, is he bound by the conventional expectations that lyric poetry must treat of love?[25] Or is it perhaps his part of a universal obligation, a universal "binding" to "reherse" the acts of Love in some universal "symposium," which has always one topic, though many speakers?

Whatever the poem's possible significance as personal, social, literary, or philosophic gesture, it introduces the book's leading idea and fundamental problem, love bound and unbound. The governing conception is already familiar from our consideration of Echo and Narcissus in *Cynthias Revels,* of Volpone, and of the characters of the *Epigrammes:* "unbound" love, though apparently "free," is sterile, inevitably destructive and self-destructive; "bound" love is the paradoxical way to true freedom, fruitfulness, and salvation. One or the other must be chosen. For Jonson as for most Renaissance writers, man is *homo amans,* and his essential, defining quality is the need and ability to love. In choosing what and how to love, he defines himself and fulfills (or fails to fulfill) his nature and destiny. Thus, the poem presents contrasting figures of bound and unbound love. Cupid escapes binding and goes (meaninglessly) "free"; that is both his volatile nature and the failure of the poet, who can find no satisfactory way to incorporate sensual desire into his work (though he does, of course, often treat it satirically). As in *Cynthias Revels,* that act of imagination or faith is beyond him (here the failure appears as a confession of his own inability rather than

---

24. Preston, "Verse Concordance," 749, lists 29 total uses of the words "love," "loves," "lover," and "lovers," of which about one quarter are verbs. One or more of these words appear in all but four of the poems (IV, VII, IX, X); and of those four, one is concerned directly with love (IX), two others tangentially so (IV, VII), and the last (X) is simply prologue to the Epode.

25. Ferry, *All in War with Time*, ch. 3.

an angry, self-righteous banishment of "giddie CUPID, VENUS franticke sonne"). The poet himself is bound in several senses. He remains himself, pedestrian, subject to age and cold, still bound to his audience, still bound, despite his failure with Cupid, to "reherse" "some act of Love." This binding, painful as it is, produces the poems that follow and the fuller, more fruitful vision of "Love" that they contain.

The first poem warns that the ensuing "numbers" will be "cold," and so they are if one defines warmth as romantic interest, the sighs and tribulations of the sonneteers. But if instead we consider other "loves," we find more concentrated warmth and vitality (beginning with "To Penshurst") than one would predict in so short a compass. The overall design (if there is one) defies easy schematization, and it is perhaps well to remember Aristotle's caution that "it is the mark of an educated man to look for precision in each class of things just so far as the nature of the subject admits."[26] One attempt has been made to see in the collection a carefully patterned symmetry of the sort frequently (and somewhat speculatively) assigned to the poetic books of Horace and others. In this reading, "To Sicknesse," the eighth poem, becomes the central axis or nadir flanked by counterpointed poems and groups of poems:[27]

```
    I    Absence of Cupid
        II-IV    Retired Virtue
                V-VII  Sexual Love
                        VIII  Nadir of Corruption/Sickness
                IX-XI  Chaste Love
        XII-XIV  Active Virtue
    XV  Presence of God
```

This is attractive and suggestive, but open to several objections. Such categories are inevitably loose and ill-fitting: III and IV do involve "retired" virtue, but "To Penshurst" is no retirement poem. Also, it is hard to imagine Jonson erecting in his mind a category for "active virtue." For Jonson (as for

---

26. Aristotle, *Nichomachean Ethics*, trans. W. D. Ross, in *Introduction to Aristotle*, ed. Richard McKeon (New York: Modern Library, 1947), 310.

27. Lauinger, "*Sylva* and Civilizing Form," Ph.D. diss., 140 ff. Although her scheme is necessarily Procrustean, her general interpretation of *The Forrest* as informed by a double concern with civility and charity has much in common with my own. Kamholtz ("Ben Jonson's Green World," 172–73) suggests a slightly different overall pattern:
    I-IV Search for, discovery, and fading of the ideal
    V-IX Erotic interlude; recovery of the ideal (IX)
    X-XI(XII) Attempts to realize the ideal
    (XII)-XV Incompleteness of these attempts
    Symmetrical counterpointings: I and XV, II and XIV, and so on.

Aristotle), virtue is either active or nonexistent. Even more damaging than specific objections, the common reader could not be expected to absorb much, if any, of such a pattern, even with repeated readings—perhaps only the counterpointing of the first and the last poems, which is obvious enough.

Rather than a scheme of static "architectural" symmetry of a sort little in evidence in Jonson's other work and practically undetectable by a reader,[28] I believe that it is more useful to think in terms of temporal rhythms: in particular, of Horace's evocative pattern of appearance, disappearance, and return, and of Jonson's own characteristic antimasque/masque rhythm. Jonson begins with an ideal of "bound" love in "To Penshurst," "To Sir Robert Wroth," and (partly) in "The Farewell for a Gentle-woman"; this is followed by examples of "unbound" love in the Farewell itself, in the poems from "Come my Celia" (V), and "To Sicknesse" (VIII). "Bound" love returns in "Drinke to me, onely" (IX) and the masterly Epode (XI), the earliest of the poems in the collection, and in a sense, the begetter of the rest, even as it is Jonson's most explicit and most memorable ideal statement of wedded love; these are followed by applications of "bound" love in the lives of two married women and a man just reaching his majority, as well as in the final psalm, "To Heaven."[29]

"To Penshurst," the best known of Jonson's longer poems, is widely interpreted as expressing Jonson's own ideal of life, a civilized, English golden age in which men and women live in hierarchical harmony with nature, the past, with other men and women high and low, and pass this way of living on to their children. The ideal is all the more vivid for defining itself against the negative background, all the things that Penshurst is "not." More than a simple opposition between dark and light, between "ambitious heaps" and this "ancient pile," the pattern repeated throughout involves three steps: what Penshurst is not, what it is, and finally what has caused it to be so. This last does not bulk as large in the telling as the first two but contains the point. Of the several schemes of order present in the poem, spatial, temporal, hierarchical, and so on, the most important is the division between outside and inside, that is, roughly, between effects and cause.[30] We are outside for the first forty-four lines, and in the description of the

---

28. But see, on Jonson's use of numerical and architectural form (particularly in the masque), Alastair Fowler, *Triumphal Forms: Structural Patterns in Elizabethan Poetry*.

29. Lauinger, Fowler, and Kamholtz, though differing in detail, all see a similar general movement.

30. For types of order in the poem, see Alastair Fowler, "The 'Better Marks' of Jonson's *To Penshurst*."

grounds, the cattle and game, the orchard, we are continually reminded that here nothing is wasted, superfluous, or unknown. Each thing has its proper use and proper season, and one can almost imagine the "painted partich" and those "officious" fishes, knowing and seeking their final use.

With the next forty-four lines, we move inside to see the cause of this natural harmony and find an evenhanded praise of the liberality and good housekeeping of the lord and his lady. Their liberality (which is not wealth merely but the proper use of what one has) evokes a universal response: "all come in" to "salute" them and to "expresse their love." This ingathering community stands in sharp opposition to those "other lords" who do not "dwell," whose houses ("built to envious show") and lives are bound to nothing and no one, and who remain isolated, self-absorbed, sterile. This lord and lady, however, have restrained their own desires and needs, and give freely to others. The binding of their self-love produces in turn the love, the sense of mutual obligation, that binds the entire community.[31] Even the speaker, a guest who has had close and embittering experience of other lords, here feels himself at home.

The last fourteen lines proceed one step further to find the cause of the social harmony.[32] It is marriage and the family, bound love once again.[33] The lady is "Noble, fruitfull, chaste withal," and the rarest (if not the greatest) of these is chastity, for chastity makes the lord's children his own and ensures that this harmonious life will not be lost, but will remain a chain of linked civility against the destructive forces of time and self-love.[34] Jonson's formulation is very close to Horace's, which was also based in the family and in

> the strength of a mind and a spirit
> properly nourished in a favored household,

---

31. James Turner notes the poem's suggestion that "wealth flows first from the landlord and not from the labourers and tenants he commands" (*The Politics of Landscape*, 144). To Marxist readers—Raymond Williams (*The Country and the City*, 32) or Don E. Wayne (*Penshurst: The Semiotics of Place and the Poetics of History*, 126), for example—such an idea seems mere mystification. But in Jonson's moral economy, ideas precede and control material facts: in restraining their own self-love, the lord and lady provide the moral capital on which the whole productive community is based.

32. Turner aptly calls the poem an "extended epigram" (*The Politics of Landscape*, 61).

33. See Isabel Rivers, *The Poetry of Conservatism*, 38: "It is through marriage and the family even more than through friendship that Jonson sees the perpetuation of social values."

34. Wayne judges this an illustration of "the extent to which portions of the aristocracy were susceptible to an infusion of bourgeois ideas and practices" (*Penshurst*, 155). More to the point, the Sidneys were English Protestants; see Ralph A. Houlbrooke, *The English Family, 1450-1700*, and Ozment, *When Fathers Ruled*.

>   the strength of Augustus' fatherly
>   affection for the children of Nero.
>   (4.4.7)

"To Sir Robert Wroth" shows Jonson practicing what he praises and keeping the ideal within the family, since Wroth was married to Lady Mary Sidney. It is a less satisfying, though perhaps not less skillful poem, Wroth having been a less satisfying man than Lord Lisle, the master of Penshurst.³⁵ The negative contrasts are longer and more prominent than at Penshurst and involve a rather full catalog of the court (3–15) and city (64–90) vices that Wroth avoids by loving and binding himself to the country and its ways.³⁶ The victory of the good life here is less complete and less secure than at Penshurst, and the speaker himself is less intimately concerned in it. Nonetheless, there are many similarities. Again we begin outdoors, but with an appropriate emphasis (Wroth was a sportsman) on hunting. Here too nothing is wasted; all is turned to harmonious use:

>   The apple-harvest, that doth longer last;
>   The hogs return'd home fat from mast;
>   The trees cut out in log; and those boughes made
>   A fire now, that lent a shade!
>   (43–46)

When we move inside to find the cause and center of this harmony we discover not lord and lady, but only Lady Mary Wroth, who is herself responsible for the "Saturnian" conjunction of freedom and delight:³⁷

>   APOLLO's harpe, and HERMES lyre resound,
>   Nor are the *Muses* strangers found:
>   The rout of rurall folke come thronging in,
>   (Their rudenesse then is thought no sinne)
>   Thy noblest spouse affords them welcome grace;
>   And the great *Heroes,* of her race,
>   Sit mixt with losse of state, or reverence.
>   Freedome doth with degree dispense.
>   (51–58)

The Sidneys freely dispense with the dignity, the pride and proper self-love

---

35. Herford and Simpson note Drummond's report of Jonson's opinion that Lady Wroth was "unworthily married on a Jealous husband" (*Conversations*, 355–56).

36. On the "masque" and "antimasque" elements in the poem, see Orgel, *The Jonsonian Masque*, 192–94.

37. Jonson not only praises her here, but also dedicated *The Alchemist* to her, and addressed her in two admiring epigrams (CIII and CV).

that is their due, and this "noblest" "loss of state" restores the primitive harmony.

The poem goes on to give extended advice to Wroth on the best means of keeping and "dwelling" in his happy "state" (ideas familiar from the *Epigrammes*) and ends with an account of God and man's relation to him that is analogous to the concluding vision of the continuous family in "To Penshurst":

> God wisheth, none should wracke on a strange shelfe:
> To him, man's dearer, then t'himselfe.
> And, howsoever we may thinke things sweet,
> He alwayes gives what he knowes meet;
> *Which who can use is happy.* Such be thou.
>
> (95-99; my italics)

This is an important passage because it is the first mention of the ultimate "bound" and binding love, God's love for man, as the cause of man's "peace"; at the same time, it concedes that human and divine judgments of "things" are not always in accord. Both elements later appear at nodal points in the book, the first as a source of anxiety in "To Heaven" (XV). The whole passage is taken from Juvenal's tenth Satire, but the italicized line has been adapted and inserted from Horace's *Odes* 4.9.45-48, in which he writes about happiness:

> non possidentem multa vocaveris
> recte beatum; rectius occupat
> nomen beati, qui deorum
>   muneribus sapienter uti

(Not the man who possesses many things may be truly called blessed; more truly the name of blessed belongs to the man who knows how to use what the gods have given wisely)

Jonson, like Horace (and unlike the translator), makes sure that the emphasis falls upon *use*. Happiness for Jonson is the proper use of things and people; proper use depends upon knowledge, and that knowledge depends upon love—even as God perfectly loves and knows men. This loving, knowing, and using are the only adequate counterpoise to the boundless and destructive greed mentioned earlier (75-90) when Jonson conjures up a scene of rampant self-love reminiscent of *Volpone:* disinheriting sires, blown up orphans and widows, heaped masses, flatterers of vice, and the omnivorous miser "brooding" over his wealth, "Not doing good, scarce when he dies" (84).

In "To the World. A farewell for a Gentle-woman, vertuous and noble," this ideal of bound love is in retreat from a world (Volpone's world) too powerful for it; it can be maintained as a consolation and possibility for the speaker alone, not for a marriage or a community. It is to this sense of virtue, embattled, weakened, disillusioned, impotent but still faithful, that we owe the fiction of the female speaker. One editor has regretted that "The lady who speaks this dramatic monologue has not been identified."[38] Yet surely she both never can be and already has been, for of course she is sister to the Celia of Volpone, the seducer alluded to in III, who will appear *in propria persona* in V, the explicit seduction that complements the many false "baits" proffered by the "world." It is the Celia who has already experienced Volpone's world and its delusive claims ("All thy good is to be sold"), meant to trap the weak and lead them to self-destruction. But unlike Volpone, she is too wise and wary to thrust her own "necke into the noose" and happily entertains no illusions about her "fraile condition," nor imagines herself separate (as Volpone had) from the human condition:

> I my state should much mistake,
> To harbour a divided thought
> From all my kinde: that, for my sake,
> There should a miracle be wrought.
> (57–60)

This firm, if tenuous, sense of connection, this bond with "kinde," enables her to maintain "shape" and perspective despite her isolation and to "make" her "peace" "Here in my bosome, and at home."

The ideal presented as fully active at Penshurst and continuing, in successively diminished forms, in the two poems that follow it disappears completely in poems V-VIII, in the two seduction songs to Celia taken wholly or in part from *Volpone,* in the jeering "That Women are but mens shaddowes," and in the sardonic "To Sicknesse."

The first song to Celia, "Come my Celia," illustrates what the "Gentle-woman" of IV complains of: the simple, plausible bait, the poisoned point beneath. The first eight lines are in the familiar, comfortable vein of *carpe diem* persuasion but are stated so simply, briefly, and neutrally that even Celia could hardly object. The next six are more challenging. Three

---

38. William B. Hunter, Jr., *The Complete Poetry of Ben Jonson*, 84.

questions suddenly make the issue more personal, more urgent, and turn what had been a reflection on the natural limitations of the self into a rejection of the binding limitations of marriage and the community. The poem ends with the well-prepared point, the fatal temptation not simply to "steale loves fruit," but to lose a transcendent sense of right and wrong, to imagine that all limits are but social impositions, and that the extinction of the self extinguishes all values in the universe. That would indeed be a miracle.

The second song to Celia is a similarly ambiguous temptation. It inverts the values found at Penshurst. This lover is secret, "wary," "covered" and takes more pleasure in the number of the kisses, the fact that they are stolen ("sweet theft"; compare Volpone's "cunning purchas"), and the envy they will provoke in others, than in the kisses themselves. This is a miser's love song, and lust as well as love gets lost in the play of the omnivorous egocentric imagination, just as when Volpone loses his opportunity with Celia through talking too much. Yet this intrinsically nasty situation is clothed in gorgeous, almost ecstatic, poetry.

"That Women are but Mens Shaddowes" is a small squib but does prepare the way for "To Sicknesse" by denigrating, although in jest, the importance of women. Women are particularly important in the poetic economy of *The Forrest* because they are the objects and agents of binding love, of marriage, of community, of poetry and humane culture.[39] One thinks of Lady Lisle, Lady Mary Wroth, the vertuous Gentle-woman, the Celia of "Drinke to me, onely," the Muse, the "Epode's" idealized Phoenix, Elizabeth, Countess of Rutland, and Katherine, Lady Aubigny. "To Sicknesse" is not the center of the book, but it is, as Lauinger calls it, the "nadir," the point at which love, poetry, and women themselves are corrupt and corrupting. The poem reeks of deliberate bad faith. Ostensibly a defense of women against "Disease," it spends most of its time describing what it claims to deplore, the "waste Livers, round about the towne" who "distill their husbands land in decoctions," who "are mann'd with ten Emp'ricks" and "entayle their loves on any." Their purpose is "to make all pleasure theirs" and the result that they "Play away, health, wealth, and fame." We have come a long way from Lady Lisle's "high huswifery" to those who waste themselves and others. The moral inversion is brilliantly underscored by the ironic, mocking narrator, whose false humility, false gallantry,

---

39. I am indebted for this point to an unpublished paper by Gabriele Bernhard Jackson, given at a special session on Jonson's poetry at the MLA convention in 1976.

specious reasoning, singsong verse, and low puns make this the height (or depth) of antimasque.

Bound and binding love return quietly, almost secretly, in the final song to Celia (IX), a poem of exquisite formal beauty.[40] Jonson uses two eight-line stanzas with alternating tetrameter and trimeter lines to achieve an effect of strength alternating with softness, action with response. The rhyme scheme is an intertwining "wreath" pattern, abcbabcb, in which the normative "b" rhyme falls on the shorter, simpler, cleaner (no caesuras until the last), "feminine" line. The sound pattern is smooth and liquid, the normative rhymes involve *i* and *e,* and the most prominent sounds within the lines are *o, n,* and *l.* The general effect is of mingled strength and quiet, or gentleness, and this mixed impression perfectly corresponds to its subject: the mutual pledging of the first stanza and the relief of "The thirst, that from the soule doth rise"; the mutual exchange of the second and its vivifying, humanizing effect. The wreath is a potent symbol of "bound" love, of the self in search of its own best fulfillment. The thirsty speaker takes the kiss from within the circle of the cup, the scent from the fragrant circle of the wreath, but in the case of the wreath he has been not only satisfied (as by the kiss), but inspired. The wreath he has sent is himself, his own soul, which hoped to find preservation but found self-forgetfulness, growth, and new life. It is one of Jonson's most evocative statements of the victory over Narcissus.

"Drinke to me, onely" is perhaps the most perfect poem in the collection, but it is the masterly Epode (XI) that most thoroughly expresses the core of Jonson's thinking. It is introduced by the untitled X, a peculiarly self-conscious dismissal of all the great names "in *Poets* heaven," which insists on the poet's "owne true fire" and "active" (one might almost say hyperactive) Muse. As one of Jonson's earliest poems (1600–1601), it could be accounted a part of the hubris that led to the pillorying of the self-styled "Horace" in the War of the Theaters. But here it serves the further purpose of reintroducing the "I" into the poems (Jonson amended "we" to "I" in the Folio), for the gradual disappearance of the ideal in poems III-VIII was accompanied by a concomitant disappearance of the poet. Now he reappears and will become increasingly active and conspicuous in poems X-XV.[41] Because the ideal is to be made explicit and active, he must appear again, as in the *Epigrammes,* to test its authenticity by his "presence" in the verse, subjecting himself to the same conditions, the same advice that he gives others.

---

40. On the background in Philostratus, see Braden, *Classics,* 166–71.
41. See Kamholtz, "Ben Jonson's Green World," 183–84.

Both X and XI were originally published in 1601 as part of Robert Chester's *Loves Martyr*.⁴² This places them at the start of Jonson's major work, about the same time he first begins to make self-love the center of attention in his work generally and, as we have seen, in *Cynthias Revels* particularly. The psychology of love presented here is very similar to that in the masque at the end of that play, being based on the stylized conflict of Eros and Anteros, of proper and improper, bound and unbound, love and self-love. Thus, the Epode is the earliest poem in *The Forrest* and is in many ways prior—logically as well as chronologically—to the rest of the collection, for it gives us the abstract statement of the moral psychology that we have been shown first in action at Penshurst. Its "displacement" to a point two-thirds of the way through enables Jonson to put it to effective use as the "masque" response to the "antimasque" poems of seduction and corruption (V-VIII). And it acts, just as ideal statements do in the masques, as a point of transition to the concluding "dance," in which the fiction opens up to include the noble spectators, who can and should enact it in their lives—here, the two married ladies (XII, XIII) and William Sidney (XIV).

The Epode has been mostly overlooked, perhaps because it has been assumed that it owes its inclusion to Jonson's desire to show that he can, among all the other forms, write an epode too. It is less vivid and less particularized than the other long poems; it seems to ramble; it is explicitly and continuously didactic; and as part of *The Phoenix and Turtle,* it has an odor of elaborate, bought-and-paid-for attitudinizing.

Some of these elements necessarily reduce the pleasure of some readers, but I think the poem deserves defense for the memorableness of what it says about true love and for the connection it demonstrates between true love and right reason. The ostensible subject is love, but what we actually learn are distinctions that make love possible. Thus we begin:

> Not to knowe vice at all, and keepe true state,
>   Is vertue, and not *Fate*:
> Next, to that vertue, is to knowe vice well,
>   And her blacke spight expell.
>   (1-4)

A very efficient opening, giving us an entire moral philosophy in four lines. As in the *Epigrammes*, one must "keepe true state." One may practice the

---

42. Herford and Simpson examine Jonson's participation in this volume (H&S 11:40–42). See also Barton's discussion of the "reappearance" of these ideas in *The New Inne* (*Ben Jonson, Dramatist,* 265–66).

virtue of innocence or experience; in either case, it is one's will rather than fate that is the determining factor. The moral psychology expounded in the next twenty-five lines describes the necessity of a wariness in separating "kind" from "unkind" experiences to prevent vice's "blacke spight" from so weakening the entire personality that "passions invade the minde, / And strike our reason blinde."[43]

This detailed attention to the movements of the soul prepares for the poem's central event, the distinction between violent and unpredictable "blinde Desire" (the Cupid who escaped the poet in I) and the experience of true Love:

> That is an essence, farre more gentle, fine,
>   Pure, perfect, nay divine;
> It is a golden chaine let downe from heaven,
>   Whose linkes are bright, and even,
> That falls like sleepe on lovers, and combines
>   The soft, and sweetest mindes
> In equal knots: This beares no brands, nor darts,
>   To murther different hearts,
> But, in a calme, and god-like unitie,
>   Preserves communitie.
>
>   (45–54)

It is a beautiful passage and beautiful in a way we have already seen, for its sound pattern is practically identical to that of "Drinke to me, onely": all *i*'s and *e*'s, *n*'s and *l*'s (except the deliberate contrast in 51–52). It contains one of Jonson's best lines: "Whose linkes are bright, and even." The eye sees the brightness of the chain from a distance and pauses, fascinated, excited, slightly tense, on the word *bright*; then the mind touches and judges the links and finds them, to our complete relief, *even*. Two of Jonson's favorite words are *bright* and *even*—the two sounds and the two experiences, perception and judgment, that determine whether one keeps true state and fulfills one's nature or fails to do so. The chain is the master image of binding love. It is like Homer's chain, of course, linking all "from the supreme God even to the bottomest dregs of the universe . . . binding at every link and never broken,"[44] and it resembles the steps of Platonic and Neoplatonic ascent from limited to ultimate beauty described in the *Sym-*

---

43. Donaldson notes the similarity to Thomas Wright's *Passions of the Mind in General* (*Ben Jonson: Poems*, 1601).

44. Hunter, *Complete Poetry*, 99, n. 12, quoting Macrobius' *Commentary on the Dream of Scipio*.

posium (and in Renaissance commentary on it). But it is also a Christian chain "let down from heaven" as an act of grace, permitting the exchange between man and God that is figured by the upward movement of lines 45–46 and the downward movement of 47 and 49. Here the ideal presented in action at Penshurst, then diminished and lost, returns in its most condensed and powerful, its most visionary form. It had been Jonson's initial insight and he makes it the climactic moment of the collection. Yet, like all visions, it is no sooner spoken than it comes under the profane attack of "some vicious foole" (66), who doubts even the possibility of such love and who, like the Volpone who scorned the "waking dreams" men value, "cryes, we dreame, and sweares, there's no such thing" (67). Jonson answers this doubt immediately in the idealized portraits of the phoenix and the turtle, innocence and experience, perfect woman and perfectible man, who can enact the vision. To do so will require above all

> A noble, and right generous mind
> (To vertuous moods inclin'd)
> That knowes the waight of guilt: He will refraine
> From thoughts of such a straine ["savage, brute affection"].
> And to his sense object this sentence ever,
> *Man may securely sinne, but safely never.*
>
> (111–16)

Poems XII and XIII turn to actual "phoenixes" and the examples provided by their personal perfections and their marriages. The first, Elizabeth, Countesse of Rutland, is the daughter of Sir Philip, the "god-like *Sidney,*" and therefore both amenable to an "offring" of poetry and one able to appreciate its value despite the "guilt" and "golden age." Having described and dismissed the "noble ignorants" who scorn poetry, Jonson moves immediately to establish its connection with love. Just as the "golden chain" of the Epode is let down from heaven, poetry provides the corresponding ascent, raising and preserving human beauty, strength, and virtue. He expresses this in terms that remind us of the previous poem:

> It is the *Muse,* alone, can raise to heaven,
> And, at her strong armes end, hold up, and even,
> The soules, shee loves.
>
> (41–43)

Like love, poetry resists time and change and provides a kind of immortality, however vicarious or artificial. Moreover, the poet is like the lover: here he speaks not only of the immortality his art will confer upon her and others, but also claims the poem will "show, how, to the life, my soule presents / Your forme imprest there" (86–87). The poem concludes with a reference to her husband and the wish (suppressed in publication when it had become known that he was impotent) that she might bear a son.

The poem to Katherine, Lady Aubigny (wife of Jonson's Penshurst-like host and benefactor, Esme, Lord Aubigny, with whom he had at some point lived for five years) alters the proportions but not the ingredients.[45] Again, poetry and married love stand out against the background of a degraded and hostile world, in which "Men are not just, [and] keepe no holy lawes / Of nature, and societie" (18–19). This lady retains, however, the virtue of wedded love "that can time, and chance defeat" (51). Her rarity in this respect is emphasized by recalling the corrupt women in "To Sicknesse" (71–88), who serve only their own pleasure, "Melt downe their husbands land," and are themselves finally "devoured" by their own vices, like Narcissus, "with his own flame wasted." Unlike the virtue of the retiring gentlewoman of IV, a virtue that merely preserves itself, this bound love is productive:

> For which you worthy are the glad encrease
> Of your blest wombe, made fruitfull from above,
>   To pay your lord the pledges of chaste love:
>   And raise a noble stemme.
>   (94–97)

At the end of the poem, Jonson unites the business of love with the business of poetry by means of a final equivocation. Early on, he had spoken of poetry as a "mirror," "subtile, cleere, refin'd, / And takes, and gives the beauties of the mind" (43–44). At the end, having spoken of her properly dependent, selfless love for her husband, he declares:

> This makes, that your affections still be new,
> And that your soules conspire, as they were gone
>   Each into other, and had now made one.
> Live that one, still; and as long yeeres doe passe,
>   *Madame,* be bold to use this truest glasse:
> Wherein, your forme, you still the same shall find;
>   Because nor it can change, nor such a minde.
>   (118–24)

"This truest glasse": is it her love or the poem? Both, I think, because both

---

45. On this poem, see van den Berg, *Action,* 132–38.

love (as Echo suggests in *Cynthias Revels*) and art (as Jonson asserts everywhere) provide "mirrors" in which the self may be truly perceived.

"To Sir William Sydney, on his Birth-day" (XIV) completes the pattern begun with "To Penshurst." After a brief (and unique) excursion outside the family, we have returned to the Sidneys with the son of the Penshurst lord and lady, who are the "authors of the feast." It is a poignant poem, and more so for the fact that the young man died the following year (1612). In him the line has failed or is at peril, not only in his death (though of course when *The Forrest* was published and probably when it was arranged, he was already dead), but in his unsteady personality. Up to this point, he had read rather haltingly "The mysteries of manners, armes, and arts" (II.98). Evidence in the Lisle letters indicates that William was thus far a pleasant but disappointing youth, who had received no significant court appointments and whose main exploit had been the stabbing of a schoolmaster.[46] Jonson's warning is serious and personal, not merely conventional. Although sensible of the warmth and good cheer, he is moved by his love for both child and parents to speak in order to promote the moral and spiritual succession that nature alone cannot and has not fully accomplished. He begins his advice:

> This day sayes, then, the number of glad yeeres
>   Are justly summ'd, that make you man;
>   Your vow
>   Must now
>   Strive all right wayes it can,
> T'outstrip your peeres:
>   Since he doth lacke
>   Of going backe
>   Little, whose will
>   Doth urge him to runne wrong, or to stand still.
>   (21-30)

The years may be "summed," but the years alone cannot "make him man" in any significant sense; that will require active striving, the binding of the self as it is, to achieve the self that can and should be, the "vertue" in the "blood." For William Sydney, his family history poses both the challenge to live up to the name and the danger of living in the name—or trying to. To underscore the latter point, Jonson recurs to the same word with which he ended "To Penshurst":

---

46. See Lisle Cecil John, "Ben Jonson's 'To Sir William Sidney on his Birth-day.'"

> For they, that swell
> With dust of ancestors, in graves but dwell.
> (39-40)

There is then a healthy and a morbid "dwelling," the vital use but also the possible corruption of the family itself, just as of love. Proper use requires the deliberate cultivation of the self in action, the "truer glass" Echo had offered to the dead Narcissus, and the advice Jonson offers to the dead (in fact, though not in the poem) William Sidney: "Then / The Birth-day shines, when logs not burne, but men." Only such action makes such days "desir'd" and makes possible a continual series of "birth-days," a perpetual resurrection of the self in action that fulfills human nature in—and in despite of—time.[47]

The pattern of "bound" love is thus completed by recognizing the necessity of *willing* its completion, and this points to the final difference with Horace. In no point are the two books more comparable than in their reliance upon particular families as living embodiments of the civility they envision. For Horace, Augustus and the Claudians are demigods, whose extraordinary heroism alone can safeguard the state and make possible a civilized life. He therefore ends his book with a celebration of Caesar's "era," in which one finds "plentiful harvests," "the ancestral way of life recalled," the empire stretched from East to West, and the state safe from "civil madness" and "hatred" (4.15.1-5). Jonson's relationship with the Sidneys is quite different, and they play a very different role in the economy of civilization presented in *The Forrest*. They are or have been poets themselves, not simply the subjects or patrons of poetry, and Jonson's praise of the life at Penshurst is not a hymn to a superior, but a debt owed to the truth. The Sidneys do not bestow a gift from above so much as they present a challenging example of a civility attained by the quiet cultivation of the self, the binding of self-love, to produce the fruit of true love, whether expressed in the life at Penshurst, in wedded love, or in poetry. These are activities which others not only benefit from, but can and should in some degree imitate.

Horace ends with the state and the family; Jonson's exploration of love goes one difficult step further, to the love of God. There is an air of inevitability about such a conclusion. As in Plato's *Symposium,* the full consideration of love begins with the lowest and ends with the highest

---

47. Kamholtz sees here a "transformation of the social event into an analogy of divine judgment" ("Ben Jonson's Green World," 191). I think the poem remains resolutely earthbound.

forms. The final address "To Heaven" provides a framing symmetry for the whole book, which, as Lauinger has observed, beginning with an explanation of the "absence of Cupid," now ends with a plea for the "presence of God." The arena of human loves and the humane culture they make possible is thus delimited both from below and from above. Moreover, turning to God at this point completes the whole by giving final consideration to what had already been mentioned elsewhere as the final cause both of true love (XI) and the good life (III).

Even if one admits the appropriateness of a "poem about God" for the end of the book, the poem is hardly what one would expect. Here is no Horatian afterglow of victory and security, no neoplatonic triumph of the mind, no resounding affirmation of Christian belief. Instead, we find a difficult, questioning, weary, dispirited poem that may well remind us, as Kerrigan observes, of Jonson's description of life as "making a little winter-love in a darke corner."[48] That he concludes with such a poem owes something, no doubt, to his habitual distrust of happy endings, a distrust evident throughout the plays and, as we have seen, in the *Epigrammes*.[49] He prefers to end this collection too with a validating crisis. Just as in the *Epigrammes* "The Famous Voyage" reminds us that at the end we remain Adam still, that self-knowledge and self-control can never be complete, so here "To Heaven" reminds us that the transformation of self-love into love, the search for love that culminates in the love of God remains, in this "state," something to be accomplished with difficulty, with doubt and self-doubt, and without a satisfactory sense of an ending.

It is crucial to recognize that the poem is a psalm. Jonson borrows at least one phrase directly ("reynes . . . hearts," Psalm 7:9) and imitates throughout the continual parallelism or "thought rhyme" characteristic of Hebrew poetry. The poem is constructed of dual and triple elements, virtuosically balanced and juxtaposed, whether of words ("good, and great"), series of words ("first, midst, and last"; "my faith, my hope, my love"; "my judge, my witnesse, and my advocate"), phrases ("wearinesse of life"; "love of thee"); lines (13 vs. 14), couplets (1–2 vs. 3–4), quatrains (1–4 vs. 5–8), and larger units (1–12 vs. 15–26). These patterns, large and small, are repeated, varied, opposed, and in their turn nested within larger patterns of synonymy, antithesis, and synthesis, forming a whole in which *this* is continually set over against *that* and "each speaks to each."

48. *Discoveries*, l. 59. Gardiner analyzes the poem as an "expression and portrait of religious melancholy" (*Craftsmanship in Context*, 72–83). The fullest discussion is Kerrigan, "Shame and Scorn."

49. Kamholtz stresses the incompleteness of the ending ("Ben Jonson's Green World").

Moreover, it is a psalm of lament, "the most abundant type . . . usually contain[ing] a statement of the poet's distress, a word of trust, an appeal to God, a declaration of the poet's obedience, and his vow to sing a Thanksgiving."[50] Save for the final element, Jonson follows this pattern closely: he states his "disease" in the first six lines and his trust ("thou art all") in the next six; he intensifies his appeal to God ("Dwell, dwell here still") in the next four and declares his painful obedience ("I know . . . I feele . . . Yet dare I not") in the last ten lines.

Yet it is a Christian psalm and a Christian lament, a Pauline meditation upon man's "state" by a mind divided between Old and New Testament senses of that state, one who "knows" and "feels" the "shame," "scorn," and "grief" of the old and at the same time believes, hopes, and desires (but does not fully possess) the new. He is aware of redemption but is not yet redeemed. He exemplifies the "Pauline paradox": "the Christian, Paul insists, lives a new life; he is a new creation; yet he must be exhorted to *be* what he *is,* to act in accordance with his new nature," because salvation "is still an end event."[51] Jonson appropriately directs our attention to both Old and New Testament texts for the sources of this meditation. In the first part, he alludes generally to the passionate "patience" of Job, for whom, in his struggle to understand his "state," God was also judge, witness, and advocate.[52] At the end of the poem, he directs us specifically to Paul's discussion of the psychology of law, sin, and grace in Romans 7 and 8, the master text for the Christian understanding of the relation of old and new dispensations. In it, Paul expounds first of all the paradox whereby the law, intended as the means of man's reconciliation with God, gives rise to and exacerbates the deadly awareness of sin and guilt:

> And the commandment, which was ordained to life,
> I found to be unto death. For sin, taking occasion
> by the commandment, deceived me, and by it slew me.
> (Romans 7:10–11)[53]

The speaker of the poem is similarly penetrated by the sense of his sinful condition:

---

50. New English Bible, headnote to the Psalms, Old Testament, 569.

51. *The Interpreter's Dictionary of the Bible*, ed. George Arthur Butterick, et al (New York: Abingdon, 1962), 3:702.

52. The several aspects of God as law occur throughout Job's speeches, most frequently as "judge" (9:15, for example), but also as "redeemer" (19:25–27). The New English Bible translates the latter term as "vindicator," "witness," and "defending counsel."

53. I quote from the Authorized Version.

> I know my state, both full of shame, and scorne,
> Conceiv'd in sinne, and unto labour borne,
> Standing with feare, and must with horror fall,
> And destin'd unto judgement, after all.
>
> (17–20)

Paul's analysis of the state or "law" of sin and death is of course preliminary to his description of the new life of the spirit that comes through Jesus Christ, and in describing these two conditions, he employs a key word ("dwell") important in this poem and earlier in *The Forrest*. Paul several times describes sin as "dwelling" within man (7:17, 18, 20) and to that opposes the "dwelling" of the Spirit of God (8:9,11). This concept is also at the heart of Jonson's poem. In which state is man to dwell? And what is to dwell within him? We may recall that in the first Sidney poem, "To Penshurst," we have seen the right sort of dwelling ("thy lord dwells"), and in the last Sidney poem, young Sir William is warned against the wrong sort of dwelling ("For they, that swell / With dust of ancestors, in graves but dwell"). At this climactic moment, Jonson himself passionately invokes the presence of God, "Dwell, dwell here still: O, being every-where / How can I doubt to finde thee ever, here?"—yet that invocation appears to go unanswered.

Most significant in this connection is Jonson's omission of the Thanksgiving, the final element of the Lament. Typically, when the psalmist has completed the presentation of his situation, there is a momentary suspense in which the soul waits for God and is answered. Psalm 22, for example, ends its appeal with

> Deliver my soul from the sword; my darling from the power of the dog.
> Save me from the lion's mouth: for thou hast heard me from the horns of the unicorns.
>
> (20–21)

It then breaks, and begins again:

> I will declare thy name unto my brethren: in the midst of the congregation will I praise thee.
> Ye that fear the Lord praise him; all ye the seed of Jacob, glorify him; and fear him, all ye the seed of Israel.
> For he hath not despised nor abhorred the affliction of the afflicted; neither hath he hid his face from him; but when he cried unto him, he heard.
>
> (22–24)

Characteristically, Jonson ends his psalm still waiting for a vision of God, still waiting for his cry to be heard, or more precisely, still waiting for the strength to apprehend and enjoy the vision that he (and everyone else) has received.[54]

Yet something has been accomplished by the end of the poem. The speaker has not yet received the presence of God, but he has prepared himself for that presence. The first two lines indicate his thoughtful ("thinke of thee"), self-absorbed melancholy ("melancholy bee"). This is the "old man," dominated by the awareness of judgment and self-judgment. But the two final lines ("or that these prayers bee / For wearinesse of life, not love of thee") respond in form and substance to the first two, replacing melancholy with prayer and thought with love. This is, if not quite the "new man," a new attitude, the proper orientation of prayerful love in which consolation and progress become possible.[55]

This final state is still painfully incomplete, but in moving from thoughtful melancholy to prayerful love, the speaker accomplishes the archetypal Jonsonian transition from self-love, the absorption in the self as it is, to love, the search for the self that can and should be. In this "state," that search is endless and endlessly repeated. Narcissus never quite leaves the pool and never quite learns who it is that he sees there. To educate him is a continual labor, for as Jonson punningly observes in *Pleasure Reconcild to Vertue,* love is not only a "maze," but a "Laborinth" in which man must work even as he wanders.[56] Yet however difficult the process, it cannot be refused, for it is human nature and destiny, and to participate in it is to grasp that "golden chaine let downe from heaven, / Whose linkes are bright, and even" (XI.47–48), to find a truth, a wisdom, that is at once the highest and yet the most intimately satisfying. As Ficino comments on Socrates' vision of the progress of love in the *Symposium*:

> True man and the Idea of man are one and the same; therefore each of us separated from God on earth is not a true man since he is separated from the Form and Idea of himself. To this Idea divine love and piety will lead us, although we are here divided and mutilated. Joined then, by love, to our own Idea, we shall become whole men, so that we shall seem first to have worshipped God in things, in order later to worship things in God; and shall seem to worship things in God in order to recover ourselves above all, and seem, in loving God, to have loved ourselves.[57]

54. See also the first three poems in the *Under-wood*.
55. Cf. Ficino, *Commentary on Plato's Symposium,* 162: "it is not knowledge of God but love of him which restores us to heaven."
56. I owe this point to Richard S. Peterson, "The Iconography of Jonson's *Pleasure Reconciled to Virtue,*" 135.
57. Ficino, *Commentary on Plato's Symposium,* 215.

EPILOGUE

Jonson's humanist educational project of a self-love purified and transformed through self-knowledge aims high but regularly acknowledges its limits. The lower limit is discovered at the end of the *Epigrammes,* the upper at the end of *The Forrest:* not the instructed and disciplined will but only grace can bring the consummation so devoutly wished. Moreover, Jonson always conceives of the cultivation of the individual's discrimination, judgment, and action as collective and communal, both in its conditions and its implications. The moral life imagined in the poetry depends upon the friendships so carefully built and maintained in the *Epigrammes* and the family celebrated in *The Forrest.* In the masques Jonson attempts to envision a wider transformation, an aim limited by the form itself and by the problematic chance of transforming its privileged spectators, the prince and his court.

This was of course part of the original conception in *Cynthias Revels,* where Jonson first rehearses as masque-maker and educator of that powerfully ambiguous "speciall fountaine of manners." Like the theater, the court is not only a place of artificial heightening of clothes and conversation, or of political and social interplay and manipulation, but also, in Jonson's hands, a potential emblem of the moral heightening that civilization makes available, in one degree or another, to all. For the poet as moralist, it poses fundamental questions in their clearest form: How would self-love express itself if it were free? Unconstrained, as a king seems unconstrained, with world enough (and money enough!) and time, what would we dream? What would we choose? What would we love?

One possibility is sketched in the thoughtless, trivial, self-loving courtiers of *Cynthias Revels*. Yet we can also imagine a darker court of self-love, as Bacon does in his interpretation of Narcissus in *De Sapientia Vetera,* comparing him to those inclined to live "with a small circle of chosen companions, all devoted admirers, who assent like an echo to everything they say, and entertain them with mouth-homage; till being by such habits gradually depraved and puffed up, and besotted at last with self-admiration, they fall into such a sloth and listlessness that they grow utterly stupid, and lose all vigour and alacrity."[1] This analysis works in two ways: politically, the prince is liable to just such an uncorrected and finally debilitating self-love; psychologically, the individual self-lover sits like a prince, at the center of personality, similarly in danger of attending only to flattering echoes. Into this "court" of self-love, whether of heedless folly or of fatal solipsism, Crites introduces the contrary possibility of an "allowable self-love" whose "place in the court of *Perfection* [is] to quicken mindes in the pursuit of honour" (*Cynthias Revels,* V.vii.29-31). The exploration and demonstration of this "true" self-love and the further definition and elaboration of the "court of Perfection" are to be one of the masques' principal concerns.

Or so Jonson may have hoped when he wrote the broad charter that opens *Hymenai* (1606), characteristically planning that his "most high, and heartie *inventions,*" "grounded upon *antiquitie,* and solide *learnings,*" will both "sound to present occasions," yet also "lay hold on more remov'd *mysteries*" (14-19). These "mysteries" are not only "above" but also potentially "within": the platonic visions of celestial harmonies wondrously realized in the "short braverie of the night" must finally hit home, not only showing the king, his courtiers and spectators the "true selves" that they can and should enact, but also implicitly showing the *readers* Jonson so eagerly anticipates (including the masquers and spectators *as readers*) how to act as "kings" in their own "courts."

Jonson brings to this complex political, social, and psychological purpose a comprehensive, multivalent analogy that runs through many of the masques: the perfection of the state is like the perfection of love. Why should love so often be the chosen metaphor and symbolic center of these "Spectacles of State"? It is of course a convenient topic for a wedding or for any entertainment that must end in a dance of lords and ladies. And the image of the fruitful marriage—suggesting the "marriage" of realms, the king's own marriage, or his "marriage" to his people—was, early in James's reign, both familiar and agreeable to a monarch whose policies centered on "union," peace, and prosperity. Yet the frequent recurrence of the question of love also reflects Jonson's conviction, expressed in *Lovers Made Men,* that

> 'Twixt eyes, tongues, hands, the mutuall strife
> Is bred, that tries the truth of life.

---

1. Bacon, *Works,* 6:705-6.

> They doe, indeed, like dead men move,
> That thinke they live, and not in love!
>
> (177-80)

A true understanding of love requires in turn a further "strife," a struggle for understanding in which crude notions or uses of love are "reformed" and "refined." Thus we see *Love Freed From Ignorance and Folly* (1611) by joining it with the king's "majestie"; or see *Love Restored* (1612), over against the competing pretensions of money, to its place at the center of imaginative and social life; or see in *A Challenge at Tilt* (1613-1614) that love, if it is to grow, requires (as Echo might well have said) both Eros and Anteros, desire and "reciprocall affection" (207-8); or see in *Lovers Made Men* (1617), how, once "follies are forgot" (217), it will be possible to "love with wit" (219); or see in *Pleasure Reconcild to Vertue* (1618) that the final test of the virtuous masquers is to dance the "maze" of love, "the subtlest maze of all" (300). And Jonson fittingly chooses to end the 1616 Folio with *The Golden Age Restor'd* (1615), a masque that involves a double restoration, recapitulating the concerns of both the *Epigrammes* and *The Forrest*. The restoration of justice requires that the "great" should be "good for their owne sake" (103), but the full and final restoration of "the *ages* libertie" requires the return of love and lovers to their original "simplicitie" (182-97).

These various displacements of antimasque by masque, of ignorant and imperfect loves by instructed and perfected ones, are all in some sense visions simply granted to Narcissus—Narcissus the king, the court, the reader—as he gazes at himself in the highly polished mirrors that the poet holds up. Their intended purpose and governing aesthetic is announced in *Love Freed*:

> How neere to good is what is faire!
> Which we no sooner see,
> But with the lines, and outward aire
> Our senses taken be.
> We wish to see it still, and prove,
> What waies wee may deserve,
> We court, we praise, we more then love.
> We are not griev'd to serve.
>
> (348-55)

But is wonder at and love of the "fair" so powerful, in itself, for good? Narcissus did not find it so; nor did Jonson in his own life; nor, finally, did the Stuart court. As Jonson frequently reminds us elsewhere, the vision of the beautiful good must be appropriated through moral perception and labor. False self-love is transformed into true self-love only by self-knowledge. Thus, in *Cynthias Revels* the "device" of "allowable self-love" is

> a *perpendicular Levell,* upon a *Cube,* or *Square.* The word, SE SUO MODULO. Alluding to that true measure of ones selfe, which . . . everie one ought to make. (V.vii.32–34)

Ovid's Narcissus was to find safety only if he never came to know himself; Jonson's will find it only if he does. Yet a true self-measure and self-knowledge requires precisely a sense of disproportion—of the painful, ridiculous gap between what we are and what we may be. As Daedalus observes of "Dauncing" in *Pleasure Reconcild,* so also more generally of the many idealizations of art, philosophy, and religion; each presents an "exercise" that

> not only shews the movers wit,
> but maketh the beholder wise,
> as he hath powre to rise to it.
> (270–72)

What is to be the source of this "powre to rise"? Jonson never solves this problem as completely in the masques as in the plays and poetic collections. For in the masque, as Stephen Orgel has said, the "scenic machine . . . *is* the action,"[2] and the moral challenges to the spectator/reader are less continuous and less direct than in other forms. Various devices are tried: increasing the proportion and weight of the antimasque, pointing to the self-consciously fictional nature of the occasion, referring obliquely to contemporary political questions, and deliberately exhorting the masquers and spectators to labor and self-restraint. All of these may conduce to the necessary "self-measure," and in the most successful of the masques, *Pleasure Reconcild* conspicuous among them, the Jonsonian experience is intact. But we know that Jonson felt at the end a frustration with "The Eloquence of Masques" (*Ungathered Verse,* XXXIV.40), a frustration that seems larger than the quarrel with Inigo Jones. For Jonson had manifestly not succeeded in educating the court as he had hoped, had not persuaded it to share even his vision of the masque, much less to *enact* the visions of perfected love those masques so often present. That enactment requires something sharper than the gorgeous dreams of the masque and something richer than the disillusioned laughter of the plays. Of the several "theaters" in which Jonson

---

2. Stephen Orgel and Roy Strong, *Inigo Jones: The Theatre of the Stuart Court,* 9. The emphasis is mine.

worked—plays, poems, and masques—it is in the poetry that he most fully controls and most powerfully realizes the central experiences that occupied him early and late, of self-love and of the potentially civilizing, transforming responses that might be made to it. It is in the poetry that he most fully expresses his view "of nature in men."

BIBLIOGRAPHY

I. PRIMARY SOURCES
A. Editions of Jonson's Work

Adams, Robert M., ed. *Ben Jonson's Plays and Masques*. New York: Norton, 1979.
Creaser, John, ed. *Ben Jonson: Volpone or the Fox*. London: Hodder and Stoughton, 1978.
Donaldson, Ian, ed. *Ben Jonson: Poems*. London: Oxford University Press, 1975.
Dutton, Richard. *Ben Jonson: Epigrams and The Forest*. Manchester: Carcanet, 1984.
Herford, C. H., and Percy and Evelyn Simpson, eds. *Ben Jonson*. 11 vols. Oxford: Clarendon, 1925-1952.
Hunter, William B., Jr., ed. *The Complete Poetry of Ben Jonson*. New York: Norton, 1963.
Johnston, George Burke, ed. *Poems of Ben Jonson*. Cambridge: Harvard University Press, 1960.
Kernan, Alvin, ed. *Volpone*. New Haven: Yale University Press, 1962.
MacLean, Hugh, ed. *Ben Jonson and the Cavalier Poets*. New York: Norton, 1974.
Newdigate, Bernard H., ed. *The Poems of Ben Jonson*. Oxford: Blackwell, 1936.
Orgel, Stephen, ed. *Ben Jonson: The Complete Masques*. New Haven: Yale University Press, 1969.
Parfitt, George, ed. *Ben Jonson: The Complete Poems*. New Haven: Yale University Press, 1982.
Parker, R. B., ed. *Volpone or, The Fox*. Manchester: Manchester University Press, 1983.
Redwine, James D., Jr., ed. *Ben Jonson's Literary Criticism*. Lincoln: University of Nebraska Press, 1970.

B. Classic and Contemporary

Aristotle. *Nichomachean Ethics*. Translated by W. D. Ross. Edited by Richard McKeon. New York: Random House, 1941.
Aubrey, John. *Lives of Eminent Men*. London: Longman, 1813.
Bacon, Francis. *Works*. Edited by James Spedding, Robert Leslie Ellis, and Douglas Denon Heath. 7 vols. London: Longman, 1889-1901.
Camden, William. *Britain*. Translated by Philemon Holland. London, 1637.
———. *Remains Concerning Britain*. 1605. Reprint. East Ardsley:EP Publishing, 1974.

Castiglione, Baldesar. *The Book of the Courtier*. Translated by George Bull. Harmondsworth: Penguin, 1976.
Coke, Sir Edward. *The First Part of the Institutes of the Laws of England. Or, A Commentary upon Littleton*. 6th ed. London, 1664.
Contarini, Gasparo. *The Commonwealth and Government of Venice*. Translated by Lewes Lewkenor. London, 1599.
Donne, John. *Poems*. Edited by Herbert J. C. Grierson. 2 vols. Oxford: Clarendon, 1912.
Ficino, Marsilio. *Commentary on Plato's Symposium*. Translated by Sears R. Jayne. University of Missouri Studies 19, no. 1. Columbia, Mo., 1944.
The Greek Anthology. Translated by W. R. Paton. 5 vols. Loeb Classical Library. London: Heinemann, 1916.
Heinsius, Daniel. *On Plot in Tragedy*. Translated by Paul R. Sellin and John J. McManmon. Northside, Calif.: San Fernando Valley State College, 1971.
Hesiod, the Homeric Hymns and Homerica. Translated by Hugh G. Evelyn-White. Loeb Classical Library. London: Heinemann, 1926.
Horace. *The Odes and Epodes*. Translated by C. E. Bennett. Loeb Classical Library. London: Heinemann, 1914.
———. *The Odes and Epodes of Horace: A Modern English Verse Translation*. Translated by Joseph P. Clancy. Chicago: University of Chicago Press, 1960.
Juvenal and Persius. Tr. G. G. Ramsay. Loeb Classical Library. Cambridge: Harvard University Press, 1969.
Kendall, Timothe. *Flowers of Epigrammes*. London, 1577.
Macrobius. *Commentary on the Dream of Scipio*. Translated by W. H. Stahl. New York: Columbia University Press, 1952.
Martial. *Epigrams*. Translated by Walter C. A. Ker. 2 vols. Loeb Classical Library. London: Heinemann, 1968.
Minturno, Antonio Sebastiano. *L'arte poetica*. 1564. Reprint. Munich: W. Fink, 1971.
The New English Bible, with the Apocrypha. Edited by Samuel Sandmel. New York: Oxford University Press, 1976.
Ovid. *Fasti*. Translated by Sir James George Frazer. Loeb Classical Library. London: Heinemann, 1931.
———. *Metamorphoses*. Translated by Frank Justin Miller. 2 vols. Loeb Classical Library. Cambridge: Harvard University Press, 1966.
Pico della Mirandola, Giovanni. "Oration on the Dignity of Man." In *The Renaissance Philosophy of Man*, edited by Ernst Cassirer, Paul Oskar Kristeller, and John Herman Randall, Jr. Chicago: University of Chicago Press, 1948.
Plato. Vol. 6. Translated by H. N. Fowler. Loeb Classical Library. London: Heinemann, 1926.
Puttenham, George. *The Arte of English Poesie*. 1589. Reprint. Menston: Scolar Press, 1968.
Ripa, Cesare. *Iconologia*. Venice: N. Pezzana, 1669.
Scaliger, J. C. *Select Translations from Scaliger's Poetics*. Translated by F. M. Padelford. New York: Holt, 1905.

Seneca. *Epistulae Morales.* Translated by Richard M. Gummere. 3 vols. Loeb Classical Library. Cambridge: Harvard University Press, 1967.
Shakespeare, William. *The Complete Works.* Edited by Alfred Harbage. Baltimore: Penguin, 1969.
Sidney, Sir Philip. "The Defence of Poesie." In *Elizabethan Critical Essays,* edited by G. Gregory Smith. Oxford: Clarendon, 1904.
Spenser, Edmund. *Poetical Works.* Edited by J. C. Smith and E. de Selincourt. London: Oxford University Press, 1912.
Statius. Translated by J. H. Mozley. 2 vols. Loeb Classical Library. Cambridge: Harvard University Press, 1969.
Tacitus. *Works.* Translated by Clifford H. Moore and John Jackson. 3 vols. Loeb Classical Library. London: Heinemann, 1931.
Valeriano Bolzani. *Hieroglyphica.* Venice, 1604.
Vives, Juan Luis. *Vives' "Introduction to Wisdom": A Renaissance Textbook.* Translated by Marian Leona Tobriner. New York: Teachers College, Columbia University, 1968.
Wright, Thomas. *The Passions of the Minde in Generall.* London, 1604.
Youll, Henry. *Canzonets to Three Voyces.* London, 1608.

II. SECONDARY SOURCES

A. Bibliographies and Concordances

Bates, Steven L., and Sidney D. Orr. *A Concordance to the Poems of Ben Jonson.* Athens: Ohio State University Press, 1978.
Brock, Dewey Heyward, and James J. Welsh. *Ben Jonson: A Quadricentennial Bibliography, 1947–1972.* Metuchen, N.J.: Scarecrow, 1974.
Di Cesare, Mario, and Ephim Fogel. *A Concordance to the Poems of Ben Jonson.* Ithaca: Cornell University Press, 1978.
Judkins, David C. *The Nondramatic Works of Ben Jonson: A Reference Guide.* Boston: Hall, 1982.
Lehrman, Walter D., Dolores J. Sarafinski, and Elizabeth Savage. *The Plays of Ben Jonson: A Reference Guide.* Boston: Hall, 1980.
Logan, Terence P., and Denzell S. Smith, eds. *The New Intellectuals: A Survey and Bibliography of Recent Studies in English Renaissance Drama.* Lincoln: University of Nebraska Press, 1977.
McPherson, David. *Ben Jonson's Library and Marginalia: An Annotated Catalogue. Studies in Philology,* Texts and Studies. Chapel Hill: University of North Carolina Press, 1974.
Preston, Michael James. "A Complete Verse Concordance to the Non-Dramatic Poetry of Ben Jonson." Ph.D. diss., University of Colorado, 1975.

B. Books and Monographs

Altheim, Franz. *A History of Roman Religion.* Translated by Harold Mattingly. London: Methuen, 1938.

Anderson, Ruth Leila. *Elizabethan Psychology and Shakespeare's Plays.* Iowa City: University of Iowa, 1927.

Atkins, John William Hey. *English Literary Criticism: The Renascence.* London: Methuen, 1955.

Auberlen, Eckhard. *The Commonwealth of Wit.* Tuebingen: Gunter Narr, 1984.

Bamborough, J. B. *Ben Jonson.* London: Hutchinson, 1970.

Barish, Jonas A., *Ben Jonson and the Language of Prose Comedy.* Cambridge: Harvard University Press, 1960.

———. *"Volpone": A Casebook.* London: Macmillan, 1972.

———, ed. *Ben Jonson: A Collection of Critical Essays.* Englewood Cliffs, N.J.: Prentice-Hall, 1963.

Barton, Anne. *Ben Jonson, Dramatist.* Cambridge: Cambridge University Press, 1984.

Beaurline, L. A. *Jonson and Elizabethan Comedy: Essays in Dramatic Rhetoric.* San Marino, Calif.: Huntington Library, 1978.

Bentley, Gerald Eades. *Shakespeare and Jonson: Their Reputations in the Seventeenth Century Compared.* 2 vols. Chicago: University of Chicago Press, 1945.

Boswell, James. *Life of Johnson.* Edited by R. W. Chapman and J. D. Fleeman. 3d ed. London: Oxford University Press, 1970.

Braden, Gordon. *The Classics and English Renaissance Poetry.* New Haven: Yale University Press, 1978.

Bradley, A. C. *Shakespearian Tragedy.* London: Macmillan, 1905.

Bradley, Jesse F. *The Jonson Allusion-Book.* New Haven: Yale University Press, 1922.

Brinkley, Roberta F., ed. *Coleridge on the Seventeenth Century.* Durham, N.C.: Duke University Press, 1955.

Brooks, Cleanth, and William K. Wimsatt. "English Neo-Classicism: Dryden and Jonson." In *Literary Criticism: A Short History.* New York: Vintage, 1957.

Brower, Reuben A. *The Fields of Light.* New York: Oxford University Press, 1951.

Bryant, Joseph A., Jr. *The Compassionate Satirist: Ben Jonson and His Imperfect World.* Athens: University of Georgia Press, 1972.

Bush, Douglas. *Classical Influences in Renaissance Literature.* Cambridge: Harvard University Press, 1952.

———. *English Literature in the Earlier Seventeenth Century, 1600–1660.* 2d ed. Oxford: Clarendon, 1962.

———. *Mythology and the Renaissance Tradition in English Poetry.* Rev. ed. New York: Norton, 1963.

———. *The Renaissance and English Humanism.* Toronto: University of Toronto Press, 1955.

Buxton, John. *Sir Philip Sidney and the English Renaissance.* London: Macmillan, 1954.

Cassirer, Ernst. *The Individual and the Cosmos in Renaissance Philosophy.* Translated by Mario Domandi. New York: Barnes and Noble, 1963.

Castelain, Maurice. *La Vie et l'oeuvre de Ben Jonson.* Paris: Hachette, 1906.

Champion, Larry S. *Ben Jonson's "Dotages": A Reconsideration of the Late Plays.* Lexington: University of Kentucky Press, 1967.

Chan, Mary. *Music in the Theatre of Ben Jonson*. Oxford: Clarendon, 1980.
Chute, Marchette. *Ben Jonson of Westminster*. New York: Dutton, 1953.
Coiro, Ann Baynes. *Robert Herrick's Hesperides and the Epigram Book Tradition*. Baltimore: Johns Hopkins University Press, 1988.
Colie, Rosalie L. *The Resources of Kind: Genre Theory in the Renaissance*. Edited by Barbara K. Lewalski. Berkeley: University of California Press, 1973.
———. *Shakespeare's Living Art*. Princeton: Princeton University Press, 1974.
Collinge, N. E. *The Structure of Horace's Odes*. Oxford: Clarendon, 1961.
Commager, H. Steele. *The Odes of Horace: A Critical Study*. New Haven: Yale University Press, 1962.
Craig, Hardin. *The Enchanted Glass: The Elizabethan Mind in Literature*. New York: Oxford University Press, 1936.
Cruttwell, Patrick. *The Shakespearian Moment*. London: Chatto and Windus, 1954.
Curtius, Ernst Robert. *European Literature and the Latin Middle Ages*. Translated by Willard R. Trask. Bollingen Series no. 36. New York: Pantheon, 1953.
Davie, Donald. *Purity of Diction in English Verse*. London: Chatto and Windus, 1952.
Debus, A. G.. *The English Paracelsians*. New York: Franklin Watts, 1966.
———, ed. *Science, Mind and Society in the Renaissance*. London: Heinemann, 1972.
Delasanta, Rodney. *The Epic Voice*. The Hague: Mouton, 1967.
De Luna, B. N. *Jonson's Romish Plot: A Study of Catiline and Its Historical Context*. Oxford: Clarendon, 1967.
De Mourgues, Odette. *Metaphysical, Baroque, and Precieux Poetry*. Oxford: Clarendon, 1953.
Dessen, Alan C. *Elizabethan Drama and the Viewer's Eye*. Chapel Hill: University of North Carolina Press, 1977.
———. *Jonson's Moral Comedy*. Evanston: Northwestern University Press, 1971.
Dick, A. L. *Paedeia Through Laughter: Jonson's Aristophanic Appeal to Human Intelligence*. The Hague: Mouton, 1974.
Donaldson, Ian. *The World Upside-Down: Comedy from Jonson to Fielding*. London: Oxford University Press, 1970.
Doran, Madeleine. *Endeavors of Art: A Study of Form in Elizabethan Drama*. Madison: University of Wisconsin Press, 1954.
Dubois, Page. *History, Rhetorical Description, and the Epic*. Cambridge: D. S. Brewer, 1982.
Duncan, Douglas. *Ben Jonson and the Lucianic Tradition*. Cambridge: Cambridge University Press, 1979.
Dunn, Esther C. *Ben Jonson's Art: Elizabethan Life and Literature as Reflected Therein*. Northampton, Mass.: Smith College, 1925.
Durling, Robert M. *The Figure of the Poet in the Renaissance Epic*. Cambridge: Harvard University Press, 1965.
DuRocher, Richard J. *Milton and Ovid*. Ithaca: Cornell University Press, 1985.
Dutton, Richard. *Ben Jonson: To the First Folio*. Cambridge: Cambridge University Press, 1983.

Eliot, T. S. *Essays on Elizabethan Drama.* New York: Harcourt, 1956.
Empson, William. *Seven Types of Ambiguity.* 3d ed. New York: New Directions, 1966.
Enck, John J. *Jonson and the Comic Truth.* Madison: University of Wisconsin Press, 1957.
Evans, Willa McClung. *Ben Jonson and Elizabethan Music.* Lancaster, Pa.: Lancaster Press, 1929.
Fergusson, Francis. *The Idea of a Theater.* Princeton: Princeton University Press, 1949.
Ferry, Anne. *All in War with Time: Love Poetry of Shakespeare, Donne, Jonson, and Marvell.* Cambridge: Harvard University Press, 1975.
Fish, Stanley. *Self-Consuming Artifacts: The Experience of Seventeenth Century Literature.* Berkeley: University of California Press, 1972.
Foakes, R. A. *The Player's Passion: Some Notes on Elizabethan Psychology and Acting.* English Association, Essays and Studies, n.s. 5, no. 7. 1954.
Fowler, Alastair. *Conceitful Thought: The Interpretation of English Renaissance Poems.* Edinburgh: Edinburgh University Press, 1975.
———. *Kinds of Literature: An Introduction to the Theory of Genres and Modes.* Cambridge: Harvard University Press, 1982.
———. *Triumphal Forms: Structural Patterns in Elizabethan Poetry.* Cambridge: Cambridge University Press, 1970.
Fowler, W. Warde. *The Roman Festivals of the Period of the Republic.* London: Macmillan, 1899.
Fraenkel, Eduard. *Horace.* Oxford: Clarendon, 1961.
Fraistat, Neil, ed. *Poems in Their Place: The Intertextuality and Order of Poetic Collections.* Chapel Hill: University of North Carolina Press, 1986.
Friedlaender, Paul. *Epigrammata: Greek Inscriptions in Verse.* Berkeley: University of California Press, 1948.
Frye, Northrop. *A Natural Perspective: The Development of Shakespearian Comedy and Romance.* New York: Columbia University Press, 1965.
Frye, Paul H. *The Poet's Calling in the English Ode.* New Haven: Yale University Press, 1980.
Furniss, W. Todd. *Three Studies in the Renaissance: Sidney, Jonson, Milton.* New Haven: Yale University Press, 1958.
Fussell, Paul, Jr. *Poetic Meter and Poetic Form.* New York: Random House, 1965.
Gardiner, Judith Kegan. *Craftsmanship in Context: The Development of Ben Jonson's Poetry.* The Hague: Mouton, 1975.
Giamatti, A. Bartlett. *Exile and Change in Renaissance Literature.* New Haven: Yale University Press, 1984.
Gilbert, Neal Ward. *Renaissance Concepts of Method.* New York: Columbia University Press, 1960.
Goldberg, Jonathan. *James I and the Politics of Literature.* Baltimore: Johns Hopkins University Press, 1983.
Gordon, D. J. *The Renaissance Imagination.* Edited by Stephen Orgel. Berkeley: University of California Press, 1975.

Greenblatt, Stephen. *Renaissance Self-Fashioning: From More to Shakespeare.* Chicago: University of Chicago Press, 1980.
Greene, Thomas M. *The Light in Troy: Imitation and Discovery in Renaissance Poetry.* New Haven: Yale University Press, 1982.
Grene, Nicholas. *Shakespeare, Jonson, Molière: The Comic Contract.* Totowa, N.J.: Barnes and Noble, 1980.
Guillen, Claudio. *Literature as System: Essays Toward the Theory of Literary History.* Princeton: Princeton University Press, 1971.
Hardison, O. B., Jr. *The Enduring Monument: A Study of the Idea of Praise in Renaissance Literary Theory and Practice.* Chapel Hill: University of North Carolina Press, 1962.
Harris, J., Stephen Orgel, and Roy Strong. *The King's Arcadia: Inigo Jones and the Stuart Court.* London: Arts Council of Great Britain, 1973.
Hegel, G. W. F. *Aesthetics: Lectures on Fine Art.* Translated by T. M. Knox. 2 vols. Oxford: Clarendon, 1975.
Helgerson, Richard. *Self-Crowned Laureates: Spenser, Jonson, Milton and the Literary System.* Berkeley: University of California Press, 1983.
Heninger, S. K., Jr. *Touches of Sweet Harmony: Psychology and Poetry.* San Marino, Calif.: Huntington Library, 1974.
Highet, Gilbert. *The Classical Tradition: Greek and Roman Influences on Western Literature.* New York: Oxford University Press, 1949.
Hollander, John. *The Untuning of the Sky: Ideas of Music in English Poetry, 1500-1700.* Princeton: Princeton University Press, 1961.
Houlbrooke, Ralph A. *The English Family, 1450-1700.* London: Longman, 1984.
Hoy, Cyrus H. *The Hyacinth Room: An Investigation into the Nature of Comedy, Tragedy, and Tragicomedy.* New York: Knopf, 1964.
Hudson, Hoyt H. *The Epigram in the English Renaissance.* Princeton: Princeton University Press, 1947.
Inglis, Fred. *The Elizabethan Poets: The Making of English Poetry from Wyatt to Ben Jonson.* London: Evans Brothers, 1969.
Jackson, Gabriele Bernhard. *Vision and Judgment in Ben Jonson's Drama.* New Haven: Yale University Press, 1968.
Jagendorf, Zvi. *The Happy End of Comedy: Jonson, Molière, and Shakespeare.* Newark: University of Delaware Press, 1984.
Johnston, George Burke. *Ben Jonson: Poet.* New York: Columbia University Press, 1945.
Keast, William R., ed. *Seventeenth Century English Poetry: Modern Essays in Criticism.* New York: Oxford University Press, 1962.
Kernan, Alvin. *The Cankered Muse: Satire of the English Renaissance.* New Haven: Yale University Press, 1959.
———. *The Plot of Satire.* New Haven: Yale University Press, 1965.
Kinsman, Robert S. *The Darker Vision of the Renaissance.* Berkeley: University of California Press, 1974.
Knights, L. C. *Drama and Society in the Age of Jonson.* London: Chatto and Windus, 1937.

Parfitt, George A. E. *Ben Jonson: Public Poet and Private Man.* London: Dent, 1976.
Parry, Graham. *The Golden Age Restor'd: The Culture of the Stuart Court, 1603-43.* New York: St. Martin's, 1981.
Partridge, Edward B. *The Broken Compass: A Study of the Major Comedies of Ben Jonson.* New York: Columbia University Press, 1958.
Paster, Gail Kern. *The Idea of the City in the Age of Shakespeare.* Athens: University of Georgia Press, 1985.
Patterson, Annabel. *Censorship and Interpretation: The Conditions of Writing and Reading in Early Modern England.* Madison: University of Wisconsin Press, 1984.
Perret, Jacques, *Horace.* Translated by Bertha Humez. New York: New York University Press, 1964.
Peterson, Richard S. *Imitation and Praise in the Poems of Ben Jonson.* New Haven: Yale University Press, 1981.
Popper, Karl. *Objective Knowledge.* Oxford: Clarendon, 1972.
Praz, Mario. *The Flaming Heart.* Gloucester, Mass.: Peter Smith, 1966.
———. *Studies in Seventeenth Century Imagery.* 2d ed. Rome: Editione di Storia e Letteratura, 1975.
Quinn, Kenneth. *Catullus: An Interpretation.* London: Batsford, 1972.
Rand, Edward K. *Ovid and his Influence.* New York: Cooper Square, 1963.
Rice, Eugene F. *The Renaissance Idea of Wisdom.* Cambridge: Harvard University Press, 1958.
Rivers, Isabel. *The Poetry of Conservatism.* Cambridge: Cambridge University Press, 1973.
Rose, Mark. *Heroic Love: Studies in Sidney and Spenser.* Cambridge: Harvard University Press, 1968.
Rosenthal, M. L. and Sally M. Gall. *The Modern Sequence: The Genius of Modern Poetry.* New York: Oxford University Press, 1983.
Rowe, George E. *Distinguishing Jonson: Imitation, Rivalry, and the Direction of a Dramatic Career.* Lincoln: University of Nebraska Press, 1988.
Saintsbury, George. *History of English Prosody.* 3 vols. New York: Macmillan, 1906-1910.
Santirocco, Matthew S. *Unity and Design in Horace's Odes.* Chapel Hill: University of North Carolina Press, 1986.
Schell, Edgar. *Strangers and Pilgrims: From The Castle of Perseverance to King Lear.* Chicago: University of Chicago Press, 1983.
Seznec, Jean. *The Survival of the Pagan Gods: The Mythological Tradition and Its Place in Renaissance Humanism and Art.* Translated by Barbara F. Sessions. New York: Pantheon, 1953.
Sharp, R. L. *From Donne to Dryden: The Revolt against Metaphysical Poetry.* Chapel Hill: University of North Carolina Press, 1940.
Sheavyn, Phoebe. *The Literary Profession in the Elizabethan Age.* 2d ed. Edited by J. W. Saunders. New York: Barnes and Noble, 1967.
Smith, Barbara Herrnstein. *Poetic Closure: A Study of How Poems End.* Chicago: University of Chicago Press, 1968.
Smith, G. Gregory. *Ben Jonson.* London: Macmillan, 1919.

Southall, Raymond. *Literature and the Rise of Capitalism*. London: Lawrence and Wishart, 1973.
Spingarn, Joel E. *A History of Literary Criticism in the Renaissance*. New York: Harcourt, 1963.
Starnes, Dewitt T., and Ernest William Talbert. *Classical Myth and Legend in Renaissance Dictionaries*. Chapel Hill: University of North Carolina Press, 1955.
Stoll, Elmer Edgar. *Poets and Playwrights*. Minneapolis: University of Minnesota Press, 1930.
Stone, Lawrence. *The Family, Sex and Marriage in England, 1500–1700*. New York: Harper & Row, 1977.
Summers, Claude J., and Ted-Larry Pebworth. *Ben Jonson*. Boston: Twayne, 1979.
———, eds. *Classic and Cavalier: Essays on Jonson and the Sons of Ben*. Pittsburgh: University of Pittsburgh Press, 1982.
Summers, Joseph H. *The Heirs of Donne and Jonson*. New York: Oxford University Press, 1970.
Sweeney, John Gordon. *Jonson and the Psychology of the Public Theater*. Princeton: Princeton University Press, 1985.
Swinburne, Algernon Charles. *A Study of Ben Jonson*. London: Chatto and Windus, 1889.
Sypher, Wylie. *Four Stages of Renaissance Style: Transformations in Art and Literature, 1400–1700*. Garden City, N.Y.: Doubleday, 1955.
Temkin, Owsei. *Galenism: Rise and Decline of a Medical Philosophy*. Ithaca: Cornell University Press, 1973.
Thayer, Calvin G. *Ben Jonson: Studies in the Plays*. Norman: University of Oklahoma Press, 1963.
Thomas, Mary Olive, ed. *Ben Jonson: Quadricentennial Essays*. Studies in the Literary Imagination 6, no. 1. April 1973.
Tillyard, E. M. W. *The Elizabethan World Picture*. London: Chatto and Windus, 1943.
Trimpi, Wesley. *Ben Jonson's Poems: A Study of the Plain Style*. Palo Alto: Stanford University Press, 1962.
Turner, James. *The Politics of Landscape*. Cambridge: Harvard University Press, 1979.
Tuve, Rosemund. *Elizabethan and Metaphysical Imagery*. Chicago: University of Chicago Press, 1947.
van den Berg, Sara J. *The Action of Ben Jonson's Poetry*. Newark: University of Delaware Press, 1987.
Vinge, Louise. *The Narcissus Theme in Western European Literature up to the Early 19th Century*. Translated by Robert Dewsnap, et al. Lund: Gleerups, 1967.
Walton, Geoffrey. *Metaphysical to Augustan: Studies in Tone and Sensibility in the Seventeenth Century*. London: Bowes and Bowes, 1955.
Watson, Robert N. *Ben Jonson's Parodic Strategy: Literary Imperialism in the Comedies*. Cambridge: Harvard University Press, 1987.
Wayne, Don E. *Penshurst: The Semiotics of Place and the Poetics of History*. Madison: University of Wisconsin Press, 1984.
Wedgwood, C. V. *Poetry and Politics under the Stuarts*. Cambridge: Cambridge University Press, 1960.

Weinberg, Bernard. *A History of Literary Criticism in the Italian Renaissance.* 2 vols. Chicago: University of Chicago Press, 1961.
Wheeler, C. F. *Classical Mythology in the Plays, Masques, and Poems of Ben Jonson.* Princeton: Princeton University Press, 1938.
White, Hayden. *Metahistory: The Historical Imagination in Nineteenth Century Europe.* Baltimore: Johns Hopkins University Press, 1973.
Wilkinson, L. P. *Horace and His Lyric Poetry.* Cambridge: Cambridge University Press, 1945.
Willey, Basil. *The Seventeenth Century Background.* London: Chatto and Windus, 1934.
Williams, Raymond. *The Country and the City.* New York: Oxford University Press, 1973.
Williamson, George. *The Proper Wit of Poetry.* Chicago: University of Chicago Press, 1961.
―――. *Seventeenth Century Contexts.* Chicago: University of Chicago Press, 1969.
Winters, Yvor. *Forms of Discovery: Critical and Historical Essays on the Forms of the Short Poem in English.* Chicago: Swallow, 1967.
Womack, Peter. *Ben Jonson.* Oxford: Basil Blackwell, 1986.

C. Articles and Essays

Anderson, William S. "The Theory and Practice of Poetic Arrangement From Vergil to Ovid." In *Poems in Their Place: The Intertextuality and Order of Poetic Collections,* edited by Neil Fraistat. Chapel Hill: University of North Carolina Press, 1986.
Babb, Howard S. "The 'Epitaph on Elizabeth, L. H.' and Ben Jonson's Style." *Journal of English and Germanic Philology* 62 (1963): 738-44.
Barish, Jonas A. "Ben Jonson and the Loathéd Stage." In *A Celebration of Ben Jonson,* edited by William Blissett, et al. Toronto: University of Toronto Press, 1973.
―――. "The Double Plot in *Volpone.*" *Modern Philology* 51 (1953): 83-92.
Beaurline, L. A. "Ben Jonson and the Illusion of Completeness." *PMLA* 84 (1969): 51-59
―――. "The Selective Principle in Jonson's Shorter Poems." *Criticism* 8 (1966): 64-74.
Bell, Ilona. "Circular Strategies and Structures in Jonson and Herbert." In *Classic and Cavalier: Essays on Jonson and the Sons of Ben,* edited by Claude J. Summers and Ted-Larry Pebworth. Pittsburgh: University of Pittsburgh Press, 1982.
Boughner, Daniel C. "Lewkenor and *Volpone.*" *Notes and Queries* 207 (1962): 124-30.
Boyd, John D. "T. S. Eliot as Critic and Rhetorician: The Essay on Jonson." *Criticism* 11 (1969): 167-182.
Bradshaw, Graham. "Three Poems Ben Jonson Did Not Write." *ELH* 47 (1980): 484-99.
Brady, Jennifer. "'Beware the Poet': Authority and Judgment in Jonson's *Epigrammes.*" *Studies in English Literature* 23 (1983): 95-112.

———. "Jonson's 'To King James': Plain Speaking in the *Epigrammes* and the *Conversations*." *Studies in Philology* 82 (1985): 380-98.
Bredvold, Louis I. "The Rise of English Classicism: A Study in Methodology." *Comparative Literature* 3 (1950): 253-68.
Brenkman, John. "Narcissus in the Text." *Georgia Review* 30 (1976): 293-327.
Brown, A. D. Fitton. "Drink to Me, Celia." *Modern Language Review* 54 (1959): 554-57.
Cain, William E. "The Place of the Poet in Jonson's 'To Penshurst' and 'To My Muse.'" *Criticism* 21 (1979): 34-48.
———. "Self and Other in Two Poems by Ben Jonson." *Studies in Philology* 80 (1983): 163-82.
Calder, Daniel G. "The Meaning of 'Imitation' in Jonson's *Discoveries*." *Neuphilologische Mitteilungen* 70 (1969): 435-40.
Carlson, Peter. "Judging Spectators." *ELH* 44 (1977): 443-57.
Clark, Ira. "Ben Jonson's Imitation." *Criticism* 20 (1978): 107-27.
Clary, Frank N., Jr. "The Vol and the Pone: A Reconsideration of Jonson's *Volpone*." *English Language Notes* 10 (December 1972): 102-7.
Cope, Jackson I. "Jonson's Reading of Spenser: The Genesis of a Poem." *English Miscellany* 10 (1959): 61-66.
Crane, Mary Thomas. "*Intret Cato:* Authority and Epigram in Sixteenth Century England." In *Renaissance Genres: Essays on Theory, History, and Interpretation,* edited by Barbara K. Lewalski. Berkeley: University of California Press, 1986.
Creaser, John. "*Volpone:* The Mortifying of the Fox." *Essays in Criticism* 25 (1975): 329-56.
Cubeta, Paul M. "Ben Jonson's Religious Lyrics." *Journal of English and Germanic Philology* 62 (1963) 96-110.
———. "'A Celebration of Charis': An Evaluation of Jonsonian Poetic Strategy." *ELH* 25 (1958): 163-80.
———. "A Jonsonian Ideal: 'To Penshurst.'" *Philological Quarterly* 42 (1963): 14-24.
Danson, Lawrence. "Jonsonian Comedy and the Discovery of the Social Self." *PMLA* 99 (1984): 179-93.
Donaldson, Ian. "Jonson's Ode to Sir Lucius Carry and Sir H. Morison." In *Ben Jonson: Quadricentennial Essays,* edited by Mary Olive Thomas. *Studies in the Literary Imagination* 6, no. 1 (April 1973): 139-52.
———. "Volpone—Quick and Dead." *Essays in Criticism* 21 (1971): 121-34.
Empson, William. "Volpone." *Hudson Review* 21 (1968-1969): 651-66.
Everett, Barbara. "Ben Jonson's 'A Vision of Beauty.'" *Critical Quarterly* 1 (1959): 238-44.
Fish, Stanley. "Authors-Readers: Jonson's Community of the Same." *Representations* 7 (1984): 26-58.
Fowler, Alastair. "The 'Better Marks' of Jonson's *To Penshurst*." *Review of English Studies* 24 (1973): 266-82.
———. "The Silva Tradition and Jonson's *The Forrest*." In *Poetic Traditions of the English Renaissance,* edited by Maynard Mack and George DeForest Lord. New Haven: Yale University Press, 1982.

Friedberg, Harris. "Ben Jonson's Poetry: Pastoral, Georgic, Epigram." *English Literary Renaissance* 4 (1974): 111-35.
Gardiner, Judith Kegan. "'A Wither'd Daffodill': Narcissism in *Cynthia's Revels*." *Literature and Psychology* 30 (1980): 26-43.
Gilbert, Allan H. "The Function of the Masques in *Cynthia's Revels*." *Philological Quarterly* 22 (1943): 211-30.
Goldberg, S. L. "Folly into Crime: The Catastrophe of *Volpone*." *Modern Language Quarterly* 20 (1959): 233-42.
Greenblatt, Stephen J. "The False Ending in *Volpone*." *Journal of English and Germanic Philology* 75 (1976): 90-104.
Greene, Thomas M. "Ben Jonson and the Centered Self." *Studies in English Literature* 10 (1970): 325-48.
———. "The Flexibility of the Self in Renaissance Literature." In *The Disciplines of Criticism: Essays in Literary Theory, Interpretation, and History*, edited by Peter Demetz, Thomas Greene, and Lowry Nelson, Jr. New Haven: Yale University Press, 1968.
Greg, W. W. "The Riddle of Jonson's Chronology." *The Library*, 4th series, 6 (1926): 340-47.
Guibbory, Achsah. "The Poet as Mythmaker: Ben Jonson's Poetry of Praise." *Clio* 5 (1976): 315-29.
Halio, Jay L. "The Metaphor of Conception and Elizabethan Theories of the Imagination." *Neophilologus* 50 (1966): 454-60.
Hallett, Charles A. "Jonson's Celia: A Reinterpretation of *Volpone*." *Studies in Philology* 68 (1971): 50-69.
Hart, Jeffrey. "Ben Jonson's Good Society: On the Growth of a Place and a Poem." *Modern Age* 7 (1963): 61-68.
Hawkins, Harriet. "Folly, Incurable Disease, and *Volpone*." *Studies in English Literature* 8 (1968): 335-48.
Heffner, Ray L., Jr. "Unifying Symbols in the Comedy of Ben Jonson." In *English Stage Comedy*, edited by W. K. Wimsatt, Jr. English Institute Essays, 1954. New York: Columbia University Press, 1955.
Helgerson, Richard. "The Elizabethan Laureate: Self-Presentation and the Literary System." *ELH* 46 (1979): 193-220.
Herendeen, Wyman H. "'Like a Circle Bounded in Itself': Jonson, Camden, and the Strategies of Praise." *Journal of Medieval and Renaissance Studies* 11 (1981): 137-67.
Herz, Judith Scherer. "Epigrams and Sonnets: Milton in the Manner of Jonson." *Milton Studies* 20 (1984): 29-41.
Hibbard, G. R. "The Country House Poem of the Seventeenth Century." *Journal of the Warburg and Courtauld Institute* 19 (1956): 159-74.
Holum, Karen J. "The Epigram: Semantic Basis for the Pointed Ending." *Linguistics* 94 (15 December 1972): 21-36.
Hoy, Cyrus. "Shakespeare, Sidney, and Marlowe: The Metamorphoses of Love." *Virginia Quarterly Review* 51 (1975): 448-58.
Inglis, Fred. "Classicism and Poetic Drama." *Essays in Criticism* 16 (1966): 154-69.
Jackson, Gabriele Bernhard. "Structural Interplay in Ben Jonson's Drama." In *Two*

Renaissance Mythmakers: Marlowe and Jonson, edited by Alvin Kernan. Baltimore: Johns Hopkins University Press, 1977.
John, Lisle Cecil. "Ben Jonson's 'To Sir William Sidney, on his Birth-day.'" *Modern Language Review* 52 (1957): 168-76.
Johnston, George Burke. "Ben Jonson of Gresham College." *Times Literary Supplement,* 28 December 1951, 837.
Kamholtz, Jonathan Z. "Ben Jonson's *Epigrammes* and Poetic Occasions." *Studies in English Literature* 23 (1983): 77-94.
―――. "Ben Jonson's Green World: Structure and Imaginative Unity in *The Forrest.*" *Studies in Philology* 78 (1981): 170-93.
Kay, W. David. "The Christian Wisdom of Ben Jonson's 'On My First Sonne.'" *Studies in English Literature* 11 (1971): 125-36.
―――. "Classicism and Complexity in Ben Jonson's Art." *Modern Language Quarterly* 43 (1982): 395-403.
―――. "The Shaping of Ben Jonson's Career: A Reexamination of Facts and Problems." *Modern Philology* 67 (1969): 224-37.
Keast, William R. "Some Seventeenth Century Allusions to Shakespeare and Jonson." *Notes and Queries* 194 (1949): 468-69.
Kernan, Alvin. "Shakespeare's and Jonson's View of Public Theater Audiences." In *Jonson and Shakespeare,* edited by Ian Donaldson. London: Macmillan, 1983.
Kerrigan, William. "Ben Jonson Full of Shame and Scorn." In *Ben Jonson: Quadricentennial Essays,* edited by Mary Olive Thomas. *Studies in the Literary Imagination* 6, no. 1 (April 1973): 199-218.
Knights, L. C. "Ben Jonson: Public Attitudes and Social Poetry." In *A Celebration of Ben Jonson,* edited by William Blissett, et al. Toronto: University of Toronto Press, 1973.
―――. "Tradition and Ben Jonson." *Scrutiny* 4 (1936): 140-57.
Leggatt, Alexander. "The Suicide of Volpone." *University of Toronto Quarterly* 39 (1969): 19-32.
Lemly, John. "Masks and Self-Portraits in Jonson's Late Poetry." *ELH* 44 (1977):248-66.
Levin, Harry. "Jonson's Metempsychosis." *Philological Quarterly* 22 (1943): 231-39.
Li, Victor P. H. "The Vanity of Length: The Long Poem as Problem in Pound's *Cantos* and Williams' *Paterson.*" *Genre* 19 (1986): 3-20.
Maclean, Hugh. "Ben Jonson's Poems: Notes on the Ordered Society." In *Essays . . . Presented to A. S. P. Woodhouse,* edited by Millar MacLure and F. W. Watt. Toronto: University of Toronto Press, 1964.
―――. "A More Secret Cause: The Wit of Jonson's Poetry." In *A Celebration of Ben Jonson,* edited by William Blissett, et al. Toronto: University of Toronto Press, 1973.
Marotti, Arthur F. "All About Jonson's Poetry." *ELH* 39 (1972): 208-37.
McDonald, Russ. "Jonsonian Comedy and the Value of *Sejanus.*" *Studies in English Literature* 19 (1981): 287-305.
―――. "Sceptical Visions: Shakespeare's Tragedies and Jonson's Comedies." *Shakespeare Survey* 34 (1981): 131-47.
McFarland, Ronald E. "Jonson's Epigrams, XI ('On Some-Thing That Walkes Some-Where')." *Explicator* 31, no. 26 (December 1972).

Medine, Peter E. "Object and Intent in Jonson's 'Famous Voyage.'" *Studies in English Literature* 15 (1975): 97–110.
Montrose, Louis Adrian. "Of Gentlemen and Shepherds: The Politics of Elizabethan Pastoral Form." *ELH* 50 (1983): 415–59.
Murray, Timothy. "From Foul Sheets to Legitimate Model: Antitheater, Text, Ben Jonson." *New Literary History* 14 (1983): 641–64.
Murrin, Michael. "Poetry as Literary Criticism." *Modern Philology* 65 (1968): 202–7.
Nash, Ralph. "Ben Jonson's Tragic Poems." *Studies in Philology* 55 (1958): 164–86.
Newton, Richard C. "'Ben./Jonson': The Poet in the Poems." In *Two Renaissance Mythmakers: Marlowe and Jonson,* edited by Alvin Kernan. Baltimore: Johns Hopkins University Press, 1977.
———. "Jonson and the (Re-)Invention of the Book." In *Classic and Cavalier: Essays on Jonson and the Sons of Ben,* edited by Claude J. Summers and Ted-Larry Pebworth. Pittsburgh: University of Pittsburgh Press, 1982.
Oates, Mary I. "Jonson's 'Ode Pindarick' and the Doctrine of Imitation." *Papers in Language and Literature* 11 (1975): 126–48.
Orgel, Stephen. "The Royal Theatre and the Role of the King." In *Patronage in the Renaissance,* edited by Guy Fitch Lytle and Stephen Orgel. Princeton: Princeton University Press, 1981.
———. "The Spectacles of State." In *Persons in Groups: Social Behavior as Identity Formation in Medieval and Renaissance Europe,* edited by Richard C. Trexler. Binghamton: Medieval and Renaissance Texts and Studies, 1985.
Palmer, D. J. "*Twelfth Night* and the Myth of Echo and Narcissus." *Shakespeare Survey* 32 (1979): 73–78.
Parker, R. B. "The Problem of Tone in Jonson's 'Comicall Satyrs.'" *Humanities Association Review* 28 (1977): 43–64.
———. "*Volpone* and *Reynard the Fox.*" *Renaissance Drama,* n.s. 7 (1976): 3–42.
Partridge, Edward B. "Jonson's *Epigrammes*: The Named and the Nameless." In *Ben Jonson: Quadricentennial Essays,* edited by Mary Olive Thomas. *Studies in the Literary Imagination* 6, no. 1 (April 1973): 153–98.
———. "Jonson's Large and Unique View of Life." In *Elizabethan Theatre IV,* edited by G. R. Hibbard. Waterloo, Ont.: Archon, 1974.
Paster, Gail Kern. "Ben Jonson and the Uses of Architecture." *Renaissance Quarterly* 27 (1974): 306–20.
Patrides, C. A. "A Poet Nearly Anonymous." In *Classic and Cavalier: Essays on Jonson and the Sons of Ben,* edited by Claude J. Summers and Ted-Larry Pebworth. Pittsburgh: University of Pittsburgh Press, 1982.
Patterson, Annabel. "Jonson, Marvell, and Miscellaneity?" In *Poems in Their Place: The Intertextuality and Order of Poetic Collections,* edited by Neil Fraistat. Chapel Hill: University of North Carolina Press, 1986.
———. "Lyric and Society in Jonson's *Under-wood.*" In *Lyric Poetry: Beyond the New Criticism,* edited by Chaviva Hošek and Patricia Parker. Ithaca: Cornell University Press, 1985.
Pearlman, E. "Ben Jonson: An Anatomy." *English Literary Renaissance* 9 (1979): 364–94.

Peterson, Richard S. "The Iconography of Jonson's *Pleasure Reconciled to Virtue*." *Journal of Medieval and Renaissance Studies* 5 (1975): 123-53.
Phelps, Gilbert. "Ben Jonson's Poetry." In *From Donne to Marvell*, vol. 3 of *A Guide to English Literature*, edited by Boris Ford. Baltimore: Penguin, 1956.
Pigman, G. W., III. "Versions of Imitation in the Renaissance." *Renaissance Quarterly* 33 (1980): 1-32.
Piper, William B. "The Inception of the Closed Heroic Couplet." *Modern Philology* 66 (1969): 306-21.
Potts, L. J. "Ben Jonson and the Seventeenth Century." *Essays and Studies*, n.s. 2 (1949): 7-24.
Prescott, Anne Lake. "The Stuart Masque and Pantagruel's Dreams." *ELH* 51 (1984): 407-30.
Rackin, Phyllis. "Poetry Without Paradox: Jonson's 'Hymne' to Cynthia." *Criticism* 4 (1962): 186-96.
Rathmell, J. C. A. "Jonson, Lord Lisle, and Penshurst." *English Literary Renaissance* 1 (1971): 250-60.
Redwine, James D. "Beyond Psychology: The Moral Basis of Jonson's Theory of Humour Characterization." *ELH* 28 (1961): 316-34.
Rollin, Roger B. "The Anxiety of Identification: Jonson and the Rival Poets." In *Classic and Cavalier: Essays on Jonson and the Sons of Ben*, edited by Claude J. Summers and Ted-Larry Pebworth. Pittsburgh: University of Pittsburgh Press, 1982.
Schelling, Felix E. "Ben Jonson and the Classical School." *PMLA* 13 (1898): 221-49.
Shapiro, Michael. "Audience Versus Dramatist in Jonson's *Epicoene* and Other Plays." *English Literary Renaissance* 3 (1973): 400-417.
Simpson, Percy. "The Art of Ben Jonson." *Essays and Studies* 30 (1945): 35-49.
Sisson, C. J. "Ben Jonson of Gresham College." *Times Literary Supplement*, 21 September 1951, 604.
Skelton, Robin. "The Masterpoet and the Multiple Tradition: The Poetry of Ben Jonson." *Style* 1 (1967): 225-46.
Slights, William W. E. "The Play of Conspiracies in *Volpone*." *Texas Studies in Literature and Language* 27 (1985): 369-89.
Smith, Bruce R. "Ben Jonson's *Epigrammes:* Portrait-Gallery, Theater, Commonwealth." *Studies in English Literature* 14 (1974): 91-109.
Southall, Raymond. "Understanding Jonson." *Essays in Criticism* 22 (1972): 83-89.
Spanos, William V. "The Real Toad in the Jonsonian Garden: Resonance in the Nondramatic Poetry." *Journal of English and Germanic Philology* 68 (1969): 1-23.
Stein, Arnold. "Plain Style, Plain Criticism, Plain Dealing, and Ben Jonson." *ELH* 30 (1963): 306-16.
Sweeney, John Gordon. "*Volpone* and the Theater of Self-Interest." *English Literary Renaissance* 12 (1982): 220-41.
Tabachnich, Stephen E. "Jonson's Epitaph on Elizabeth, L. H." *Explicator* 29 (1971), item 77.
Talbert, Ernest William. "The Classical Mythology and the Structure of Ben Jonson's *Cynthia's Revels*." *Philological Quarterly* 22 (1943): 193-210.

———. "New Light on Ben Jonson's Workmanship." *Studies in Philology* 40 (1943): 154-85.
Thomson, Patricia. "The Literature of Patronage." *Essays in Criticism* 2 (1952): 267-84.
Thron, E. M. "Jonson's *Cynthia's Revels:* Multiplicity and Unity." *Studies in English Literature* 11 (1971): 235-47.
Toliver, Harold. "Householding and the Poet's Vocation: Jonson and After." *English Studies* 66 (1985): 113-22.
Underhill, Hugh. "Kinds of Seriousness in Poems by Ben Jonson and Jon Silkin." *Ariel* 10, no. 4 (October 1979): 57-67.
Venuti, Lawrence. "Why Jonson Wrote Not of Love." *Journal of Medieval and Renaissance Studies* 12 (1982): 195-220.
Vickers, Brian. "Epideictic and Epic in the Renaissance." *New Literary History* 14 (1983): 641-64.
Walker, Ralph S. "Ben Jonson's *Discoveries*." *Essays and Studies*, n.s. 5 (1952): 32-42.
———. "Ben Jonson's Lyric Poetry." *Criterion* 12 (1933-1934): 430-48.
———. "Literary Criticism in Jonson's Conversations with Drummond." *English* 8 (1951): 222-30.
Watson, George. "Ramus, Miss Tuve, and the New Petromachia." *Modern Philology* 55 (1958): 259-62.
Wayne, Don E. "Poetry and Power in Ben Jonson's *Epigrammes:* The Naming of Facts or the Figuring of Social Relations?" *Renaissance and Modern Studies* 23 (1979): 79-103.
Weld, John S. "Christian Comedy: *Volpone*." *Studies in Philology* 51 (1954): 172-93.
Whipple, T. K. "Martial and the English Epigram from Sir Thomas Wyatt to Ben Jonson." *Modern Philology* 10 (1925): 279-314.
Wiersma, Stanley M. "Jonson's 'To John Donne.'" *Explicator* 25 (1966), item 4.
Williams, Kathleen. "Milton, Greatest Spenserian." In *Milton and the Line of Vision*, edited by Joseph A. Wittreich, Jr. Madison: University of Wisconsin Press, 1975.
Wilson, Edmund. "Morose Ben Jonson." In *The Triple Thinkers: Twelve Essays on Literary Subjects*. Rev. ed. New York: Oxford University Press, 1948.
Wilson, Gayle Edward. "Jonson's Use of the Bible and the Great Chain of Being in 'To Penshurst.'" *Studies in English Literature* 8 (1968): 77-89.
Wiltenburg, Robert. "'What need hast thou of me? or of my *Muse*?': Jonson and Cecil, Politician and Poet." In *The Muses' Commonweale*, edited by Claude J. Summers and Ted-Larry Pebworth. Columbia: University of Missouri Press, 1988.
Winner, Jack D. "Ben Jonson's *Epigrammes* and the Conventions of Formal Verse Satire." *Studies in English Literature* 23 (1983): 95-112.
Woods, Susanne. "Ben Jonson's Cary-Morison Ode: Some Observations on Structure and Form." *Studies in English Literature* 18 (1978): 57-74.
Wykes, David. "Ben Jonson's 'Chast Booke': The *Epigrammes*." *Renaissance and Modern Studies* 13 (1969): 76-87.

Young, R. V., Jr. "Jonson, Crashaw, and the Development of the English Epigram." *Genre* 12 (1979): 137-52.

———. "Style and Structure in Jonson's *Epigrammes*." *Criticism* 17 (1975): 201-22.

Zender, Karl F. "The Unveiling of the Goddess in *Cynthia's Revels*." *Journal of English and Germanic Philology* 77 (1978): 37-52.

D. Dissertations

Early, Robert Schafer. "Ben Jonson's *Epigrammes:* A Study in Convention." Ph.D. diss., Rutgers University, 1972.

Humez, Jean McMahon. "The Manners of Epigram: A Study of the Epigram Volumes of Martial, Harington, and Jonson." Ph.D. diss., Yale University, 1972.

Langvardt, Arthur Leroy. "The Verse Epigram in England During the Sixteenth and Early Seventeenth Centuries." Ph.D. diss., University of Colorado, 1956.

Lauinger, Ann Jacobson. "The *Sylva* and Civilizing Form in Ben Jonson's *The Forrest*." Ph.D. diss., Princeton University, 1977.

Miller, Richard Henry. "Diverse Unity: Ben Jonson's *Epigrammes* Considered Individually and Collectively." Ph.D. diss., Columbia University, 1972.

Newton, Richard Coleman. "Foundations of Ben Jonson's Poetic Style: *Epigrammes* and *The Forrest*." Ph.D. diss., University of California, Berkeley, 1970.

INDEX

Anderson, William S., 96*n*17
Aristotle, 20, 106-7

Bacon, Francis, 4-5, 66, 73; "Of Nature in Men," 1-4; "Of Friendship," 43; "Narcissus," 124-25
Barish, Jonas, 14*n*29
Barton, Anne, ix, 32*n*23, 52*n*15, 114*n*42
Beaurline, L. A., 19*n*36, 25*n*7, 34*n*25
Beauty, use of, 12-14, 33
Bedford, Lucy Harington, Countess of, 73, 77, 82-83
Bonds of identity, 27, 29-30, 32, 39, 44, 105, 108-12, 118. *See also* Friendship; Love; Marriage; Self-love
"Book" of poems: *Epigrammes,* 48-50; *The Forrest,* 92-94, 106-7; in Horace, 95-99
Brady, Jennifer, 67*n*49
Bush, Douglas, 12*n*27, 90

Camden, William, 60-61, 70, 72, 73, 81
Castiglione, Baldesar, 91
Cecil, Robert, Earl of Salisbury, 72-76
Chan, Mary, 12*n*28
Coke, Sir Edward, 66
Collinge, N. E., 96
Contract, 65-72, 84, 89
Creaser, John, 31*n*22
Custom, 3, 66

Danson, Lawrence, 23*n*4
Dante, 37, 91
Dessen, Alan C., 30*n*18
Donne, John, 71, 81-82
Durling, Robert M., 59, 70*n*54
Dutton, Richard, 75*n*62
Dwelling, 119, 122

Echo: in Jonson, 7-15; in Ovid, 8
Eliot, T. S., 19
Empson, William, 26, 42*n*34

Epic, 59-61, 85. *See also* Gall, Sally M.; Hegel, G. W. F.
Epigram: manner and speaker of, 46-47, 51, 70, 84; dignity of, 50-51, 61-63, 87; form and dynamics of, 56-58, 61-63, 87
Evil: nature of, x, 26; imagination of, 35-37, 44; representation of, 88-90. *See also* Metamorphosis; Self-love

Fergusson, Francis, 20
Ferry, Anne, 105
Ficino, Marsilio, 123
Fish, Stanley, 2*n*5, 55*n*21
Fowler, Alastair, 62*nn*38,39, 94*n*10, 107*nn*28,30
Fraistat, Neil, 64*n*43
Friedberg, Harris, 76*n*64
Friedlaender, Paul, 63*n*42
Friendship, 43, 81-84, 124

Gall, Sally M., 63-64
Gardiner, Judith Kegan, 19*n*35, 46*nn*4,5, 71*n*55
Giamatti, A. Bartlett, 86*n*79
Greenblatt, Stephen, 32*n*24
Greene, Thomas M., 3*n*7, 24, 28*n*14, 38*n*27, 66*n*46, 78*n*67

Hallett, Charles A., 31*n*22
Hawkins, Harriet, 24, 29*n*16
Hegel, G. W. F., 62-63
Helgerson, Richard, 59*n*27
Herford, C. H., 6, 59-60
Holum, Karen M., 57*n*25
Horace: in *Poetaster,* 5; *Odes IV,* 94-99; contrasted with Jonson, 94-95, 101-4, 119; as artist, 96, 103-4, 107; and *The Forrest,* 100-101
Human nature: in Bacon, 1-4, 15; in Jonson, 8, 9, 14, 15, 19-20, 86-87, 123, 128; defined in action, 10
Humez, Jean, 47

Humors, 34

Jackson, Gabriele Bernhard, 2n3, 5, 11n25, 30n20, 112n39
James I, 65, 76n63
Johnson, Samuel, 1
Jonson, Ben: dramatic vs. nondramatic form, ix, 19-20, 29, 44, 87-90, 127-28; as artist, x, 14, 19-25 passim, 31, 34, 40, 43-48 passim, 76, 87-90, 93, 120; as moralist, xi, 31, 38, 40, 83, 88-90, 114, 119, 127; motto, 17; poet's role, 21-22, 75-77, 89-90; endings, 22, 40, 42-43, 84-85, 119-20, 122-23; laughter in, 39; relation to audience, 44, 86-87, 90; Workes (1616), 45, 92, 100; Conversations with Drummond, 57, 60, 73; masques, 91, 124-28; as translator of Horace, 103-4

Plays and masques
—*The Alchemist*, 22, 24, 58
—*Bartholmew Fayre*, 58, 87
—*Catiline*, 48, 65, 74n60
—*Cynthias Revels*, ix, 5-20, 23, 43, 64, 87-88, 91, 105, 114, 124-25
—*Every Man in His Humour*, 50, 58
—*Hymenai*, 125
—*Love Freed From Ignorance and Folly*, 126
—*Lovers Made Men*, 126
—*The Magnetic Lady*, 88
—*Pleasure Reconcild to Vertue*, 92, 127
—*Poetaster*, 5, 94
—*Volpone*, x, xi, 5, 20, 21-44, 62n39, 64, 70, 79, 88, 89, 110-11

Poems and prose
—*Discoveries*, 4-5
—*Epigrammes*, xi, 5, 20, 21, 45-90, 92, 100-101, 124; I, 48-49; II, 57, 76; III, 67; IV, 67; V, 67; IX, 70; XI, 70; XII, 58; XIV, 71, 72; XVIII, 50, 71; XXI, 90; XXII, 71; XXIII, 71, 81; XXV, 69-70; XL, 22, 60n30; XLIII, 73; XLV, 46, 71; LXIII, 73; LXIV, 74; LXV, 72-77, 84, 86, 87; LXX, 77-78; LXXVI, 73, 82-83; XCIV, 82, 83; XCV, 79-81; XCVI, 81-82; CI, 83-84; CII, 53, 55, 65, 69, 78; CXVIII, 79; CXXVIII, 78; CXXXIII, 84-87
—*The Forrest*, xi, 5, 92-123, 124; I, 100, 104-6; II, 107-9, 111, 118; III, 100, 109-11; IV, 111; V, 111-12; VI, 112; VII, 112; VIII, 112-13; IX, 113; X, 100, 113-14; XI, 47, 107, 113-16; XII, 100, 116-17; XIII, 116, 117-18; XIV, 100, 118-19; XV, 46, 100, 110, 120-23;

—*Heroologia*, 60, 61; "Queen and huntress," 15-17; "Slow, slow, fresh fount," 12-14
—*Underwood*, 93, 104; XLIII, 22; XLVI, 66; LI, 4; LXXXVI, 102-4
—*Ungathered Verse*: XXXIV, 127
Judgment, 4, 40, 44; subject to imagination, 35-37; in *Epigrammes*, 58, 66-67

Kamholtz, Jonathan Z., 93n9, 101n21, 106n27
Kernan, Alvin, 24
Kerrigan, William, 46n4, 120
Knights, L. C., 24

Lauinger, Ann Jacobson, 94n10, 106n27, 112, 120
Leggatt, Alexander, 25n8, 39n29
Lessing, G. E., 57
Lewis, C. S., 91
Loewenstein, Joseph F., 6n17, 8n21, 19n36
Love: fundamental in Jonson, ix, 105; as "mirror" of self, 10-11, 117-18; Jonson's critique of, 91. *See also* Self-love

Marriage, xi, 108, 125; and family, 99. *See also* Sidney family
Martial, 23, 49-56, 57
Martz, Louis L., 70n54
Maus, Katherine Eisaman, 40n32, 86n79, 89n84, 91n3
Medine, Peter E., 86n78
Metamorphosis, 14, 27-28, 69-70, 79
Milton, John, 89
Minturno, Antonio Sebastiano, 62
Montaigne, 45
Musgrove, S., 23n4

Names and naming, 51-53, 58, 60, 76-77, 81
Narcissus: in Ovid, 6-7, 8, 127; in Jonson, 7-15, 84, 126-27; in Bacon, 124-25
Nature: vs. fortune, x, 23-29, 33; man's place in, 1-2, 64, 128
Nelson, Lowry, Jr., 3n6
Nietzsche, Friederich, 96

Orgel, Stephen, 45n1, 127
Otis, Brooks, 5n13, 7
Ovid: in *Poetaster*, 5; on Narcissus and Echo, 6-7, 8, 14; contrasted with Jonson, 11, 127
Ozment, Steven, 27n12, 108n34

Parker, R. B., 25n8, 26n9, 32n23, 40n31

Index

Partridge, Edward B., 24, 45*n*2, 47, 53, 65*n*44, 68*n*50
Pastoral and anti-pastoral, 26–27
Patterson, Annabel, 27*n*13, 45–46*n*2, 104*n*23
Pembroke, William Herbert, Earl of, 53, 55, 65, 69
Peterson, Richard S., 56*n*22, 65, 86*n*77, 123*n*56
Petrarch, 91
Pico della Mirandola, 3*n*7
Pigman, G. W., 56*n*22
Plato: *Cratylus*, 52–53, 81; *Symposium*, 115–16, 119, 123
Pope, Alexander, 17
Preston, Michael James, 53*n*18, 67*n*48, 105*n*24

Rivers, Isabel, 108*n*23
Roe, William, 77–78
Rosenthal, M. L., 63–64

Santirocco, Matthew S., 49*n*11, 96*n*15
Savile, Sir Henry, 79–81
Schell, Edgar, 29*n*17, 44*n*38
Self-knowledge, 7, 11, 18, 39, 84, 87, 90, 124, 127; flight from, 17; incompleteness of, 119
Self-love: new idea, ix; centrality in Jonson, x, 19, 44, 64, 92; transformation of, x–xi, 89, 92, 124, 127, 128; binding of, xi, 92, 108, 119; disruptive effects of, 7, 30, 44; true or "allowable," 17, 18, 123, 125, 127; and self-deception, 34, 70; incompletely transformed, 120, 123. *See also* Bonds of identity; Love; Narcissus

Seneca, 17, 77–78
Shakespeare, William, 37, 88–89, 93
Sidney, Sir Philip, 56, 80
Sidney, Sir Robert, Lord Lisle, 109, 118
Sidney, Sir William, 118–19
Sidney family, 100, 109–10, 119, 122
Smith, Bruce R., 47, 76*n*65
Southall, Raymond, 83*n*74, 92*n*4
Spanos, William V., 16, 96*n*18
Spenser, Edmund, 10, 91
Standing, 78–79. *See also* Metamorphosis
Starnes, Dewitt T., 8, 10*n*24
Statius, 94
Summers, Joseph H., ix, 81*n*72, 89*n*83
Sweeney, John Gordon, 34*n*26, 38*n*28
Swinburne, A. C., 24, 46, 84

Talbert, Ernest William, 8, 10*n*24
Thayer, Calvin G., 8, 15
Turner, James, 108*nn*31,32

van den Berg, Sara J., 85*n*76, 94*n*11, 117*n*45
Vinge, Louise, 6*n*14, 8*n*21, 12*n*27
Virgil, 5, 72, 77–78
Vives, Juan Luis, 17

Wayne, Don E., 53*n*17, 108*nn*31,34
Weld, John S., 24, 26*n*9, 30*n*18
Williams, Raymond, 27*n*11, 92*n*4, 108*n*31
Wilson, Edmund, ix–x, 68*n*51
Wroth, Lady Mary, 109, 112
Wroth, Sir Robert, 109–10
Wykes, David, 47

Youll, Henry, 12*n*28